Defence Reform in Croatia and Serbia-Montenegro

Timothy Edmunds

Routledge
Taylor & Francis Group

LONDON AND NEW YORK

ADELPHI PAPER 360

First published October 2003 by **Oxford University Press** for
The International Institute for Strategic Studies
Arundel House, 13–15 Arundel Street, Temple Place, London WC2R 3DX

This reprint published by Routledge
2 Park Square, Milton Park, Abingdon, Oxon, OX14 4RN
For the International Institute for Strategic Studies
Arundel House, 13-15 Arundel Street, Temple Place, London, WC2R 3DX
www.iiss.org

Simultaneously published in the USA and Canada
By Routledge
711 Third Avenue, New York, NY 10017

Routledge is an imprint of the Taylor & Francis Group, an informa business

© The International Institute for Strategic Studies 2003

Director John Chipman
Editor Tim Huxley
Copy Editor Matthew Foley

British Library Cataloguing in Publication Data
Data available

Library of Congress Cataloguing in Publication Data

ISBN 0-19-853039-0
ISSN 0567-932x

Contents

Introduction

On 12 March 2003, Zoran Djindjic, Serbia's reformist prime minister, was murdered by assassins from the Special Operations Unit (JSO), a semi-autonomous element of the Serbian security services closely connected to organised crime. Djindjic's assassination has illustrated the continuing legacy of the Milosevic period in Serbia-Montenegro, in particular the damage that might be caused by armed organisations able and willing to intervene in domestic political change.[1]

At the time of the fall of Slobodan Milosevic in 2000, the most significant of these groups in Serbia-Montenegro was the Army of Yugoslavia (VJ). Its leadership was packed with Milosevic cronies, its institutional interests appeared to be directly threatened by post-authoritarian change, and it had a history of playing an autonomous political role within the state. Many of these features were mirrored in Croatia. Here, the armed forces (OSRH) had also been politicised, with the leadership closely tied to the authoritarian regime of President Franjo Tudjman and his nationalist Croatian Democratic Union (HDZ) party. As in Serbia-Montenegro, the OSRH's own institutional interests appeared to be deeply threatened by political change. Between 2000 and 2003, questions relating to the transformation of the VJ and OSRH have been central to wider processes of post-authoritarian and post-conflict transition in both these countries. Moreover, despite some important differences in scale and context, both have faced a series of common challenges in this area.

For both countries, the space for change opened in 2000, in the wake of a decade of conflict and authoritarianism. Croatia fought a desperate and often brutal war for independence between 1991 and 1995, and intervened in the conflict in neighbouring Bosnia-

Herzegovina during the same period. Tudjman and the HDZ dominated domestic politics, and contributed to the country's isolation from the European political mainstream. In the Federal Republic of Yugoslavia (FRY), Milosevic presided over a corrupt and dictatorial regime. The country entered a series of destructive and bitter conflicts, resulting in international condemnation, sanctions and, in 1999, military action by NATO in Kosovo. In both states, this situation fundamentally changed in 2000. Tudjman died in December 1999, and early the following year the HDZ was roundly defeated by a reformist coalition in parliamentary and presidential elections. In FRY, October 2000 saw the electoral defeat and eventual ousting of Milosevic by the Democratic Opposition of Serbia (DOS) coalition.

These events introduced new personalities and new politics into the former Yugoslav region, and created important new opportunities for post-authoritarian governments. For the first time since the days of the Socialist Federative Republic of Yugoslavia (SFRY), democratisation and the prospect of reintegration into the European mainstream appeared possible. Nonetheless, the transitions in Croatia and Serbia-Montenegro have also been accompanied by significant challenges. These have included the need to implement and consolidate new democratic political arrangements; the need for each state to come to terms with the legacy of conflict, particularly war crimes; the need to reform domestic institutions, structures and constitutional arrangements; and the need to build new relationships with neighbours in Southeastern Europe and beyond.

In both states, defence reform is a key feature of all these processes. In both countries, new governments have had to establish and consolidate democratic and civilian control of their armed forces. Moreover, the armed forces of both states are confronted with the need to adapt to a radically-changed security environment and to a modern system of oversight. However, in both Croatia and Serbia-Montenegro changing domestic priorities have led to sharp falls in defence budgets, which means that these challenges must be faced in the context of significant reductions in available resources.

The defence reform processes of Croatia and Serbia-Montenegro are also closely linked to the demands and priorities of the international community. Both countries have identified closer integration with NATO and the Partnership for Peace programme (PfP) as foreign policy priorities. The security-oriented nature of these organisations has placed defence reform questions at the forefront of Croatia and Serbia-Montenegro's rapprochement with the West almost by default. In addition, the highly-sensitive issue of war crimes and cooperation with the International Criminal Tribunal for the former Yugoslavia (ICTY) directly affects both states' armed forces, and asks fundamental questions of their defence reform processes.

Many aspects of these defence reform challenges parallel those faced by post-Communist Central and Eastern Europe in the early 1990s. Here too the armed forces were politicised and closely linked to the old authoritarian order. They were also faced with a radically changed security environment, the need to either radically reform their force structures in response to this or create new ones from scratch, and the need to adapt to radically reduced defence budgets. Across Central and Eastern Europe, the prospect of NATO enlargement in particular also gave the international community an important role in shaping the nature and direction of post-Communist defence reform.[2] Over this period, the Central and Eastern European states have made significant progress in addressing these defence reform challenges. Indeed, ten of them have now either joined or been invited to join the NATO alliance.

A key concern of this paper is the extent to which the largely successful defence reform experiences of the wider post-Communist region are transferable to Croatia and Serbia-Montenegro today. Has the experience of conflict and the unique features of these two countries' experiences in the 1990s simply delayed the common demands of post-authoritarian defence transition, or do the armed forces of Croatia and Serbia-Montenegro face a different series of challenges entirely? In particular, will international institutions such as NATO be able to exert a similarly strong influence over the way in which these countries' defence reforms develop? Or will the legacy of war crimes, sanctions, international exclusion and – in the case of Serbia-Montenegro at least – NATO bombing prove more difficult obstacles to overcome?

This paper assesses the factors shaping the nature and direction of defence reform in Croatia and Serbia-Montenegro. In doing so, it is informed by the defence reform experiences of Central and Eastern European, which since the early 1990s have focused around three thematic areas. The first of these is the institution of democratic, civilian control of armed forces. This has been an important feature of post-Communist democratisation more widely, not least because armed forces themselves are powerful domestic actors and have the potential to interfere in domestic political change – particularly if, as was the case in Central and Eastern Europe under communism or in Croatia and Serbia-Montenegro under Tudjman and Milosevic, their interests were tied to those of the old order.

The second theme of this paper is structural and organisational military reform. Again, this has been a key element of all the post-Communist defence reform processes, and is also of central importance in understanding the challenges currently faced by Croatia and Serbia-Montenegro. Military reform is linked to the first theme in that democratic and civilian control of armed forces is important not only as a mechanism for restraining the praetorian or undemocratic intervention of the military in domestic politics, but also as a fundamental component of how states conduct their defence planning. This in turn addresses questions of what the roles of armed forces actually are in the provision of state security, and how best they should be organised, structured and funded. These are key elements in any process of defence reform, and loom particularly large at times of major political or geostrategic change, when the armed forces themselves often have to undergo significant organisational reform.

Finally, the paper addresses the role of the international community – particularly the countries of the Euro-Atlantic region – in encouraging these processes. Across the former Communist region, this has been a definitive factor in shaping the manner in which both democratic civil–military relations and military reform plans have been prioritised and implemented. In Croatia and Serbia-Montenegro, Western countries and institutions have attempted to encourage reform through the provision of defence assistance and the application of pre-conditionality and direct conditionality. As such, understanding the influence of the West in relation to these issues – and how this interacts with domestic factors – is of crucial importance to understanding the defence reform process more widely.

Before examining these themes in more detail, it is necessary to summarise the role of the armed forces in Croatia and Serbia-Montenegro during the 1990s. This is important because it provides the underlying context against which the changes of 2000–03 have taken place, without which many of the key features in the Croatian and Serbia-Montenegrin defence reform processes cannot be fully understood.

Defence reform in Croatia

The Croatian defence sector has been in transition since 1991, passing through three phases that have paralleled the development of the Croatian state itself: formation during the war years of 1991–95; authoritarian consolidation between 1995 and 2000; and democratisation from 2000 onwards.[3] In this respect, the OSRH is no stranger to the challenges and demands of reform and change. However, since the death of Tudjman and the defeat of the HDZ, Croatia's defence sector has entered a new, qualitatively different phase of transformation. Defence reform today presents new opportunities for both the armed forces and the Croatian state more widely. The post-conflict, post-authoritarian rehabilitation of Croatia into the European mainstream is well under way, and closer integration with institutions such as the European Union (EU) and NATO is one of the principal goals of Croatian foreign policy. Croatia joined NATO's PfP programme in May 2000, and full NATO membership is a distinct possibility in the medium term. Defence reform issues are centrally important in this context. Croatia perceives NATO membership as a first step towards wider European integration, particularly membership of the EU. Successful implementation of key defence reforms meets the pre-conditionality demands of NATO accession, and so gives the OSRH a special significance in the country's foreign policy.

The OSRH was established in the first years of Croatia's war of independence at the beginning of the 1990s.[4] At this time, the fledgling Croatian state was fighting for survival against a well-equipped conventional military in the form of the Yugoslav People's Army (JNA), as well as Yugoslav-sponsored Serbian secessionist movements and paramilitary organisations in Krajina and Slavonia. In contrast, the foundations for the future OSRH were rudimentary, given that Croatia did not have a long tradition of having its own armed forces, beyond the lightly armed Territorial Defence (TO) forces of the Yugoslav period. Croat representation in the JNA officer corps had always been disproportionately low; when coupled with the JNA's successful withdrawal from its Croatian facilities with almost all of its heavy weaponry in November 1991, this ensured that Croatia faced the task of building its armed forces both under fire, and to all intents and purposes from scratch.[5] In practice, the OSRH was constructed on the basis of civilian volunteers, militarised units from the republican police force, locally-based TO forces and a small number of former JNA officers whose loyalties lay with Croatia.[6] In addition, during the first phase of the war, Croatia was placed under an international arms embargo, which meant that what weaponry it could obtain was often stolen, fought for, or smuggled in.

From these desperate circumstances in the early 1990s, the OSRH was able to build itself into an effective fighting force. It intervened controversially in the war in Bosnia in support of Bosnian Croat forces in 1991–95, and in 1995 launched the offensive operations *Flash* and *Storm*, which regained most of the Croatian territory that had been lost to the Serbs.[7] This transformation was made possible by the ease with which the Tudjman regime was able to flout the arms embargo, the tacit support of Western governments – who saw Croatian rearmament as a useful counter to Serbian aggression – and the provision of technical support and training by organisations such as the US-based firm Military Professional Resources Incorporated (MPRI).[8] The OSRH also had a specifically political role, and was used as a key legitimating element of the HDZ regime's brand of nationalist isolationism.

In addition to the OSRH's politicisation during the authoritarian period, its involvement in conflict between 1991 and 1995 – and the manner in which that conflict was conducted – has left an important legacy for the Croatian defence reform process today. A number of former OSRH officers and personnel have been indicted for war crimes by the ICTY on the basis of their actions during the war, and the question of cooperation with the tribunal remains highly sensitive in both the armed forces and among the Croatian public more widely. This is significant not just because it goes to the heart of Croatia's rehabilitation, but also because it is a key feature of its evolving relationship with Western institutions such as NATO and the EU.

Defence reform in Serbia-Montenegro

The period since 1991 has also brought fundamental and continuing changes for the army in Serbia-Montenegro.[9] As in Croatia, these changes have passed through three broad phases. The first occurred between 1991 and 1995. This was the initial period of the collapse of the SFRY, during which the old JNA – from 1992 split into the VJ and the Bosnian Serb Army of Republika Srpska (VRS) – was engaged in an essentially pro-Serb struggle to preserve the Yugoslav federation. The second phase occurred between 1995 and 2000, and was characterised by authoritarian consolidation. During this time, the VJ became increasingly co-opted by the Milosevic regime. It was subject to a series of purges amongst its officer corps, was heavily engaged in the Kosovo conflict and was bombed by NATO in 1999. The final phase is the post-authoritarian period from 2000 onwards. This has for the most part been characterised by stagnation in relation to defence reform, caused by uncertainty over the future of the Yugoslav federation and obstruction from among the army leadership. However, there were important personnel changes in the Army General Staff in 2002, while February 2003 saw the finalisation of a new constitutional Charter that transformed the FRY into the State Union of Serbia and Montenegro (SUSM), and the VJ into the army of Serbia and Montenegro (VSCG). Taken together, these developments have provided new momentum to defence reform, and suggest that this post-2000 malaise in relation to defence reform may at last be coming to an end.

The character of the changes experienced by the army in Serbia-Montenegro during these phases has been different from those of the Croatian OSRH. First, the VJ/VSCG is not essentially a new formation. Its origins lie in the traditions, structures and history of the old JNA. Moreover, as the VJ it was a central actor in the events surrounding the disintegration of Yugoslavia, and as the VSCG its future remains closely linked to the changing constitutional shape of the state. These legacies inform the institutional culture of the army itself, and present particular barriers to, and opportunities for, reform.

The VJ/VSCG, and the JNA before it, was always an explicitly *federal* and (as the JNA) *pan-Yugoslav* organisation – albeit one with a strong Serbian flavour in the officer corps. For Tito, from the late 1960s onwards, the JNA was the guarantor of the Yugoslav federal state. This was formalised by constitutional changes in 1971 and 1974, which gave the JNA an explicitly political role, and allocated it equal status with the two autonomous provinces of Vojvodina and Kosovo in the Central Committee of the Yugoslav League of Communists. This effectively made it a ninth partner in the SFRY.[10] As a consequence, the JNA was left in a difficult position when faced with the nationalist upheavals in Yugoslavia in the early 1990s. On the one hand, its political and constitutional role placed it in natural opposition to the secessionist republics of Slovenia and Croatia – a situation which ultimately led to its co-option by the Milosevic regime and the Serbian nationalist cause. On the other, however, while its officer corps was increasingly dominated by Serbs, it remained a professional institution at its core, with a tradition of corporate self-governance.[11] Ultimately, however, as Miroslav Hadzic observes: 'the Army could not save the country it belonged to and so in order to survive it had to lean towards the one that Milosevic offered'.[12]

The JNA/VJ's military effectiveness in the Yugoslav conflict was limited, and it was expelled from Slovenia in 1991, Croatia in 1995 and Kosovo in 1999 – though in the latter case there is a widespread perception in Serbia that the army had performed as well as it could against overwhelming odds. The VJ was indirectly involved in the conflict in Bosnia through the provision of technical, personnel and material support to the Bosnian Serb VRS, and contacts between the two armies remained close throughout the Milosevic period. In most cases, the VJ's wartime conduct in the 1990s was better than many other organisations in the Yugoslav security sector. Most atrocities were carried out by semi-official (often locally recruited) paramilitary groups, special units and Serbian Interior Ministry formations. Nonetheless, VJ special forces units in particular were certainly involved in some of the more brutal aspects of the conflicts in Croatia, Bosnia and Kosovo, numerous former members of the VJ have been indicted by the court at The Hague, and the question of cooperation with the ICTY remains a key feature of the defence reform process in Serbia-Montenegro.[13]

Since 2000, the army has maintained a particularly strong connection with the federal government of Serbia-Montenegro. Between 2000 and 2003, for example, the defence budget accounted for around two-thirds of the FRY's total federal spending – almost all of which was in practice collected exclusively from the Serbian republic. Since 2000, therefore, the fate of the army and the fate of the Yugoslav federation have been closely and inextricably linked. This in turn has contributed to the inertia in Serbia-Montenegro's defence reform process in this period, making the army's future role, the direction of its reforms and the shape of its civil–military legislation difficult to judge while the fate of the federation itself has remained undecided. The introduction of the new constitutional arrangement has provided a more predictable context in which defence reform can take place. Nonetheless, the VSCG retains its special federal position in the new state, and its future development remains closely linked to the evolving relationship between the Serbian and Montenegrin republics.

Chapter 1

Democratic and Civilian Control of Armed Forces

The relationship of the armed forces with domestic politics is of central importance during post-authoritarian transitions. The concentration of coercive power in the military's hands makes it an important domestic actor, with the potential to influence or even frustrate the political process. This is particularly the case if the military had been politicised under the previous authoritarian regime, or if its institutional interests were closely linked to the old order. As a consequence, the establishment and consolidation of civilian control over armed forces is an important feature of most post-authoritarian transitions, and it has been one of NATO's key concerns in its efforts to encourage defence reform in the former Communist region.

In states undergoing democratisation, it is also important to distinguish between *civilian* control of armed forces, and their *democratic* control. Civilian control is a necessary element of democratic control, but on its own it is not sufficient. Indeed, democratic models of civil–military relations entail much more than the simple maximisation of civilian power over the armed forces. They also involve the effective governance of the defence sector in a framework of clear constitutional responsibilities and transparency. This in turn relates to four key areas: first, legally-defined institutional responsibilities and relationships, which place the armed forces under clear civilian control; second, the depoliticisation of armed forces and the removal of their influence in domestic politics; third, mechanisms for the effective, transparent and accountable implementation of defence policy and the defence budget; and finally, the wider engagement of civil society in defence matters.[1]

Croatia, 2000–03

The Croatian defence sector has always been under strong civilian, if not especially democratic, control. During the Tudjman period, this was exercised through three main instruments. The first was the establishment of chains of command and responsibility that allowed the president to bypass many of Croatia's constitutional provisions for civilian control, and personally direct the development and operations of the armed forces. This complemented the strong system of presidential control laid out in the constitution, which identified the president as the Commander-in-Chief of the armed forces. Thus, Tudjman created two presidential bodies that exploited constitutional loopholes and his own extensive executive powers to enable him to circumvent both parliament (the *Sabor*) and the law. The first of these was the Strategic Decisions Council (VSO), an *ad hoc* advisory body convened by presidential invitation. The VSO was created in order to weaken any dissent from within the regime itself, and provide a veneer of legality to any extra-legal decisions by Tudjman across a range of issues, but with a particular focus on economic and financial matters.[2] The second was a dedicated defence and security body, the Defence and National Security Committee (VONS), whose members the president appointed personally and which effectively allowed him to side-step parliamentary scrutiny or control. As a consequence, throughout much of the 1990s key elements of the Croatian security sector, including the OSRH, were to all intents and purposes answerable to the presidency alone, while the presidency in turn was largely accountable to no-one.

A second component of Tudjman's system of civilian control over the defence sector was politicisation. Despite the fact that, constitutionally, the OSRH was identified as firmly apolitical, tendrils of the HDZ's organisation penetrated it throughout. During the formation of the armed forces at the beginning of the 1990s, many of the key positions in the military were filled by HDZ officials rather than military professionals, in order to encourage both party control and military loyalty. These arrangements were later institutionalised, so that appointment to high positions within the military – or indeed promotion at any level – became increasingly dependent on HDZ membership.[3] Similarly, Tudjman loyalists were appointed to key positions within the Ministry of Defence and the General Staff in order to ensure that the entire chain of command over the OSRH would be politically reliable. There was also a Political Directorate within the Ministry of Defence, and at every level of command in the OSRH there was a Deputy Commander for Political Affairs.[4] In effect, this system created an often informal pyramid of clientalism and political influence, where HDZ interests would be represented at every level of the promotion system, and through which strong political influence could be exercised.

In addition to executive control and politicisation, there was also a system of material incentives, which allowed key personnel to enrich themselves and gain social prominence as long as they toed the party line. OSRH officers were often the first to take over property that had been abandoned by Serbs during the war, the defence budget was subject to massive embezzlement and fraud, and trusted personnel were awarded with high rank or a stake in Tudjman's privatisation process.[5] Underpinning these three mechanisms of civilian presidential control was the legitimacy of the regime itself, maintained by its identification with Croatian nationalism and its apparent adherence to democratic principles.[6]

The victory of the anti-HDZ coalition in the January 2000 elections illustrated that the democratic trappings of Tudjman-era Croatia were not wholly superficial, particularly in relation to the position of the military. Indeed, for all its politicisation and penetration by the HDZ regime, and despite significant political activity by pro-HDZ generals at the time and pressure on military personnel to vote for the HDZ, the OSRH remained in its barracks during Croatia's political transition. Despite this, the legacy of the Tudjman era ran deeply in Croatia, and since forming the new government in 2000, the six- (and from June 2001, five) party coalition under Prime Minister Ivica Racan has faced a series of challenges in establishing and consolidating democratic control over the defence sector. In common with much of the rest of post-Communist Europe, these challenges have often had as much to do with the civilian bureaucratic and attitudinal legacies of the Tudjman period as they have with the praetorian concerns of post-authoritarian civil–military relations.

Since 2000, Croatia has taken significant steps towards the institution of democratic control over the OSRH. Structures and mechanisms for democratic control have largely been established, and the principle of civilian control has been consolidated and shown to be effective; chains of command have been restructured; and politicisation questions have begun to be addressed. Given the context in which it has had to work, the government's achievements in these areas should not be underestimated. Nonetheless, Croatia continues to wrestle with difficult problems in relation to the democratic control of its defence sector. These fall into three main categories. First, there is continuing confusion over chains of command and responsibility, resulting from political and institutional rivalries between and within the government, the *Sabor*, the Ministry of Defence and the presidency. Second, a legacy of politicisation and clientalism persists, which remains open to abuse and, on occasion, has allowed civilian politicians to exploit the defence sector in support of their own partisan or personal agendas. Finally, there have been capacity problems related to the ability of the state and society to play their proper role in Croatia's new system of civil–military relations. These particularly concern issues of transparency and oversight; the civilianisation of the defence bureaucracies and the development of civilian expertise more widely; resourcing problems; and the involvement and engagement of civil society groups in defence and security issues.

An unwieldy constitution

The Racan government has used a modified version of Croatia's 1990 constitution as the basis for establishing democratic control over the OSRH. While containing a basically sound foundation for democratic civil–military relations, the constitution is also replete with overlapping responsibilities and ambiguities in relation to the defence sector. It was amended in November 2000 with the aim of diluting the previously strong position of the presidency. Broadly, these amendments established Croatia as a parliamentary democracy, with executive power resting primarily in the hands of the government, which in turn is responsible to the *Sabor*.[7] However, in relation to matters of national security, the amended constitution retains an additional strong role for the presidency, making the incumbent 'responsible for the defence of the independence and territorial integrity of the Republic of Croatia' as well as the Commander-in-Chief of the armed forces.[8] While this division of responsibilities is not inherently unworkable or undemocratic, it is unwieldy and unclear as to where exact institutional responsibilities lie. In practice, therefore, its provisions remain open to interpretation, and it relies on close cooperation between the three branches of government to be effective.[9] Given the rivalries within Croatia's ruling coalition, achieving a satisfactory level of cooperation has often been difficult. This in turn has had a negative impact on the workability of the country's mechanisms for democratic defence policymaking in practice.

This situation is illustrated by the time it has taken to introduce important clarifications of Croatia's defence and security legislation, identified as a priority from 2000 onwards. These were only approved by the *Sabor* in March 2002, more than two years after the change of government. They consist of two strategies and four new laws: the National Security Strategy and the Defence Strategy; and the Defence Act, the Law on Service in the Armed Forces, the Law on the Participation of Members of the Croatian Armed Forces in Peace Operations Abroad and the Law on the Production, Repair and Traffic in Weapons and Military Equipment. The delay in the introduction of the legislation resulted from infighting, suspicion and mistrust between the government and the presidency over the extent of their various institutional powers and responsibilities. Indeed, President Stipe Mesic has been keen to preserve the presidency's defence-related roles – not least because these make up a sizable proportion of the president's suite of powers – and has viewed many of the government's actions in this area as both unconstitutional and politically motivated.[10] For its part, the government has wanted to concentrate defence-related responsibilities in its own hands on the basis of Croatia's negative experience of centralised presidential power during the Tudjman period.

One consequence of this rivalry has been that the new legislation remains a compromise, and retains a series of complicated institutional inter-relationships and ambiguities. For example, the government must propose the appointment or dismissal of the Chief of General Staff. The *Sabor* also has an input in the matter, and the president actually carries out the appointment or dismissal.[11] Even more problematic is the role of the minister of defence in the chain of command. According to the Defence Law, the president exercises his commanding authority through the minister. However, because the government is constitutionally responsible to the *Sabor* rather than to the presidency, the president is unable either to appoint or dismiss the defence minister, but can only offer an opinion on their suitability for the job. In the case of a serious clash of interests between the president and the defence minister, the president must ask the *Sabor* to dismiss the minister, and until parliament reaches a decision is able to exercise direct command of the armed forces through the Chief of General Staff.[12] Some observers suggest that in practice, this gives the president the opportunity to misuse the power of his office, rather than the authority to carry out his function as Commander-in-Chief effectively.[13]

Depoliticisation

Since taking office in 2000, the new government has faced the task of neutralising HDZ influence within the defence sector and implementing a restructuring process to consolidate its mechanisms for democratic control of the military. This drive has resulted partly from Croatia's wider democratisation process, but also from the perceived requirements and demands of closer integration with NATO and the EU.[14] Then Defence Minister Jozo Rados signalled his aim in 2000, when he dismissed seven deputy defence ministers and declared:

> We intend to discontinue the practice of political activity within the Croatian Army ... officers and civil servants within the Ministry of Defence will be allowed to belong to political parties but not to hold party functions. Our aim is to have experts in key positions of the Ministry of Defence.[15]

Tudjman's own First Guards regiment – which fell outside the OSRH's normal chain of command – was disbanded, and a number of other officials within the Ministry of Defence were dismissed or pensioned off.[16] In addition, the *Sabor* ratified a government measure on increased cooperation with the ICTY, a move which exposed several military personnel, some of them senior, to possible arrest and transfer to The Hague.[17]

The implementation of these changes has not been without resistance from within the OSRH. On 12 September 2000, 12 suspects, including two OSRH generals, were arrested on suspicion of war crimes. The move enraged the HDZ opposition, which in turn helped to organise opposition within the OSRH. Soon after the arrests, seven serving and five retired generals, including a deputy Chief of General Staff, a former Chief of General Staff and Inspector-General of the OSRH, wrote an open letter to the government, attacking its policies and criticising its 'slandering of war heroes'. In response, Mesic moved swiftly in support of the government by pensioning off all the serving generals who had signed the letter.[18]

In acting so decisively, Mesic established an important precedent of civilian control over the armed forces, which has largely remained in place since. However, the HDZ continues to influence defence and security policy in Croatia, at least indirectly. A further legacy of the Tudjman period was the creation of strongly pro-HDZ veterans' associations. The largest, the Association of Veterans and Invalids of the Patriotic War (HVIDRA), was established by the HDZ in order to bolster its nationalist legitimacy. Since 2000, it has pursued a campaign of criticism and obstruction towards the government's defence reforms. In 2000, it organised a series of protests and roadblocks in protest at Croatia's cooperation with the ICTY. These were repeated in March 2003, when a Croatian court sentenced former General Mirko Norac to 12 years in jail for the killing of at least 50 Serb civilians in 1991.[19]

While the impact of these actions was ultimately limited by their lack of sustained public support, veterans' associations like HVIDRA continue to wield significant influence over defence policy. Senior policy-makers admitted in 2002 that nervousness over the reaction of the veterans' associations had helped to stall the implementation of some reforms, such as downsizing in the OSRH.[20] The veterans' associations have a particular influence on the ICTY issue, where they tap into a far wider popular unease over the question of Croatian responsibility for war crimes. In the latter part of 2002, these associations were prominent advocates of the government's refusal to transfer former General Janko Bobetko to The Hague. In doing so, they helped to mobilise popular feeling on the issue and ensure that any climbdown on the transfer would be politically costly to the government and beneficial to the HDZ. Indeed, when Mesic called for Croatia to 'keep its word' to the international community and suggested that Bobetko should be handed over to the ICTY, veterans' groups and the HDZ called for his impeachment.[21]

The legacy of politicisation goes deeper than simple HDZ influence, with some observers in Zagreb noting that HDZ networks within the OSRH have been replaced by others based around new political and personal centres of power.[22] Their implication is that promotion and advancement in the Ministry of Defence in particular is still often based on personal connections and political sympathies rather than fitness for the post. Certainly, the potential for abuse remains. The defence minister, for example, appoints nine assistant ministers who are each responsible for the administration of particular departments in the ministry. These are explicitly political appointments with party affiliations, who in turn are responsible for appointments and promotions within their own departments. In many ways, this mirrors practices in many established democracies such as the US. Nonetheless, given the politically divided nature of Croatia's current coalition it has potentially negative implications for the politicisation and effectiveness of the country's defence policymaking. Some insiders suggest that there are significant politically-motivated tensions between departments of the Ministry of Defence, and that as a result personnel have often been prevented by their departmental heads from consulting outside of their immediate directorate, even on areas of strong mutual interest.[23]

Undoubtedly, a degree of politicisation persists within Croatia's defence structures. However, senior figures in the Ministry of Defence and elsewhere argue that this is not as widespread as many critics allege, and that the ministry itself is working hard to eliminate it. For example, former Defence Minister Rados stated in 2002 that, while there might be bad practice at some levels in Croatia's defence system, this resulted less from explicitly party political reasons than from problems associated with adaptation to a radically different system of managing human resources. He also noted that the Ministry of Defence had established clear objective rules for promotions across the board, and that in many respects he considered it safer for his staff to declare their political allegiances than pretend that such allegiances did not exist.[24] In addition, the nature of the governing coalition has meant that a certain decentralisation and diffusion of party political power has been inevitable, simply because the spoils of office have had to be shared amongst the different members.

Transparency, oversight and expertise

Rados's assertion that the Ministry of Defence's problems stem from issues of institutional adaptation rather than from more overt questions of politicisation points to a wider challenge in Croatia's civil–military relations. This concerns the deeper institutional legacies of the Tudjman and Communist periods, where structures for civilian control of the armed forces and the management of defence were organised around authoritarian procedures and norms. Key elements of a system of democratic control, such as transparency and oversight, were not present to any appreciable degree. As other post-Communist experiences have illustrated, implementing institutional and legal reforms is only a first step, and needs to be followed by a longer-term attitudinal and behavioural change in the way that the defence sector conducts its business.[25]

For example, and despite many notable exceptions, there is often a lack of appropriate expertise in the Ministry of Defence. This results both from the particular history of the ministry itself, and from the reforms of the new administration. Under Tudjman, promotion within the OSRH generally occurred either on the basis of HDZ affiliations, or 'in the field' through experience gained at a tactical level during the war. This has had two consequences. The first is that OSRH officers appointed to administrative positions in the Ministry of Defence sometimes do not have the appropriate education or experience to enable them to carry out their jobs effectively.[26] The second is that objective career records and assessments are generally absent, making it difficult for the new administration to assess the quality and experience of existing staff, except on the basis of their own observations.[27]

A key aim of the new government has been to civilianise the Ministry of Defence. This has been identified by both the new government and by NATO as a key element in the consolidation of civilian control over the military. However, given the closed nature of the defence establishment during both the Tudjman and the Communist periods, this has meant that many new civilian personnel often have limited experience and expertise in defence issues. Additionally, the political nature of many appointments in the ministry means that, if a department head leaves, so also do many of the staff underneath them, with a detrimental impact on the ministry's developing pool of expertise. While problems of this kind exist in many large institutions, they have a particular relevance in the Croatian defence sector because the existing pool of relevant civilian experience and expertise is already so small.

If limited capacity is a problem in the Ministry of Defence, its impact is even greater in relation to the *Sabor*'s ability to provide effective oversight and scrutiny of defence issues. Under Tudjman, the *Sabor* was almost completely segregated from the defence sector, and today its role remains similarly limited.[28] To a large degree, this results from a lack of interest and expertise in security matters amongst parliamentarians, and a lack of resources to adequately support their scrutiny functions. The *Sabor* does have a parliamentary committee for Internal Affairs and National Security (UPNB), but even its members admit that its remit is very broad, and its impact limited and beholden to party politics.[29] Moreover, for many Croatians defence issues are understandably of a much lower priority than other areas of policy, such as economic reform or the social services, and this is reflected in low levels of interest in these issues in parliament. General Pavao Miljavac, a former defence minister and member of the UPNB committee, noted in 2002 that most parliamentarians 'do not want to listen' when defence and security are mentioned.[30]

This lack of parliamentary interest and expertise has had a negative effect on the *Sabor*'s ability to question and scrutinise defence policy. For example, while the information parliament receives on the defence budget is generally comprehensive – and updated by a governmental interim report every six months – in practice the degree to which this can be properly probed and questioned is limited. Those involved in the process observe that inadequate time is devoted to consideration of budgetary issues, and that often parliamentarians, even those in the UPNB committee, do not fully understand the implications or detail of the report. Moreover, party political disagreements on budgetary issues are often resolved long before legislation reaches parliament for approval.[31] As a consequence, the *Sabor* has generally been happy to follow advice from the Ministry of Defence on defence questions, a passive approach that has limited its power of oversight to little more than a 'rubber stamp' for government policy.

Throughout Croatia's structures for management and oversight of the defence sector, problems of state capacity are reinforced by a lack of resources. For example, the ability of the Ministry of Defence to manage its finances is hampered by inadequate accountancy software and computer technology.[32] In the *Sabor*, parliamentarians complain about their lack of support staff, such as researchers, and their limited access to briefing papers, library resources and other material. Croatian policymakers are open about the need for investment in these areas, and this is slowly beginning to occur in areas such as education programmes for Ministry of Defence personnel and parliamentarians. But in practice the scope is limited by restrictions in the defence budget and the prioritisation of other areas of defence spending.

Civil society

During the Tudjman period, the engagement of civil society in defence matters beyond the activities of the HDZ-sponsored veterans' organisations was limited. While there were important exceptions, in the main these issues were almost exclusively the domain of cadres within the OSRH and the HDZ. The Tudjman regime disbanded many defence-oriented courses at Croatia's universities, such as Zagreb University's Defendology course at its Faculty of Political Science. Non-governmental analysis of defence issues was often censored, and media comment on defence matters was extremely limited.[33]

Since 2000, civil society engagement has expanded significantly. Undergraduate and postgraduate courses in Defendology have been reintroduced at Zagreb University and two defence-related think-tanks, the Centre for Defendological Research (CDI) and the Institute for International Relations (IMO), have been established or reinvigorated. Both have begun to engage with the Croatian defence establishment. The CDI has organised a series of international conferences on civil–military relations, which have attracted high-level cooperation and interest across the Croatian defence sector. The Faculty of Political Science has designed its Defendology course explicitly to prepare students for careers in the security sector ministries.[34] Moreover, the Croatian government has made an effort to utilise non-governmental defence expertise in its reform efforts. For example, an independent team of academics and experts was commissioned by the government to prepare a Study on National Security as the basis for Croatia's new security legislation and strategies.[35] The development of university courses that address defence issues as part of their syllabus may eventually be part of a long-term solution to the 'expertise deficit' in Croatia's defence and security structures.

However, despite the depth of involvement the impact on policy of this civil society engagement is questionable. For example, the team which drafted the widely-respected Study on National Security complain that many of their recommendations have not been included in the new legislation.[36] Moreover, civil society's engagement with defence issues does not appear to extend much beyond a small circle of Zagreb-based experts and institutions. Observers complain that there is a limited number of experienced defence correspondents in the Croatian media, and that, when defence and security issues are reported, it is often in a sensationalist manner or dominated by reports of scandals or the polemics of veterans' organisations and the HDZ.[37] This situation is changing – stimulated in part by popular interest in potential NATO membership – and to a degree represents a lack of popular interest in such 'expert' reporting that might be expected in any country. But nonetheless, defence remains rather a low priority in the Croatian media's portfolio of interests.[38]

Serbia-Montenegro, 2000–03

For most of the Milosevic period, the JNA/VJ was not subject to the same degree of civilian control as was the OSRH under Tudjman. Indeed, the army was not a natural ally of Milosevic, who never wholly trusted its traditions of professional and political autonomy and its constitutional linkage to the federal state, rather than to the regime. As a consequence, throughout the 1990s Milosevic attempted to undermine the JNA/VJ's professional and political autonomy and subjugate it to his own control. In doing so, he utilised three main strategies.

The first, in common with the approach adopted by Tudjman in Croatia, was the establishment of new chains of command and responsibility over the army that bypassed or manipulated the FRY's existing constitutional provisions for civil–military relations. Under Yugoslavia's 1974 constitution, command responsibility over the army lay in the hands of the federal presidency. Given that, between 1990 and 1997, Milosevic was president of the Serbian republic rather than the federal state, these arrangements would have given him no formal authority over the army. However, the 1992 constitution of the newly proclaimed FRY altered these arrangements and established a Supreme Defence Council (VSO) comprising the FRY, Serbian and Montenegrin presidents, which would exercise ultimate command over the military.[39] This gave Milosevic, as both the Serbian and subsequently federal president, a new and constitutionally sanctioned mechanism for exercising control over the VJ.[40]

The second strategy through which Milosevic established his control over the army was through personnel changes and by purging the officer corps. This began with the resignation or early retirement of many non-Serbs from the JNA in the early 1990s.[41] As well as this Serbianisation, the JNA's evolution into the VJ provided an opportunity for the Milosevic regime to target politically-unreliable elements of the officer corps. Throughout 1992–93, many of the remaining JNA officers in the VJ were either dismissed or forced into early retirement in a programme of purges which left only nine former JNA generals in the whole institution, and eliminated any vestiges of old-style 'Yugoslavism' in the new VJ.[42] Even then, the VJ continued to exhibit what for Milosevic was a worrying degree of autonomy, and it was only in 1998, when Milosevic loyalist General Dragoljub Ojdanic was appointed Chief of the General Staff, that he consolidated his personal control over the VJ's leadership.[43]

The final way in which Milosevic undermined the influence of the VJ was through the development of direct institutional competitors from other elements of the Yugoslav security sector. In particular, Milosevic initiated a significant militarisation of the Serbian police forces (MUP), and encouraged the development of semi-autonomous special forces and paramilitary organisations outside the army's normal chain of command.[44] These alternative military formations forced the VJ to compete for favour and funding from the regime in Belgrade, and functioned as an alternative power-base for Milosevic should the army prove unreliable.[45]

Despite these moves, the VJ did not in the end intervene to save Milosevic in the wake of his defeat in the October 2000 presidential elections. Nonetheless, the legacy of his policies towards the army has been lasting, and Serbia-Montenegro has faced considerable challenges in the implementation of democratic mechanisms for its civil–military relations. As in Croatia, these challenges have increasingly less to do with any praetorian threat that the military may pose to the new regime, and more to do with the need to overcome the structural and attitudinal legacies of the Milosevic period.

Since October 2000, Serbia-Montenegro has embarked on a tentative process of democratising its civil–military relations. Partly because of the war crimes issue and the political importance that the government has placed on joining the PfP, civil–military reform has become a growing political priority in Belgrade, and there have been a number of positive developments in this area. In particular, the principle of civilian control over the VSCG has been established; the government has, after some delay, implemented important personnel changes in the army's Milosevic-era leadership; and the federal parliament has introduced new legislation relating to the management and control of the defence sector. However, Serbia-Montenegro continues to face a number of problems in the consolidation of its civil–military arrangements. These fall into four main categories. The first has concerned uncertainty over the future shape and character of the Yugoslav federation, which has stalled the development of new defence legislation and allowed confusion and ambiguity to persist in some areas of civil–military relations. The second factor has been serious political rivalries within the Democratic Opposition of Serbia (DOS) coalition, which took power after the fall of Milosevic. These rivalries have at times led civilian politicians to politicise key defence reform questions and attempt to exploit the army for partisan purposes. The third factor has concerned the continuing problem of outspoken Milosevic-era appointments in the VJ leadership. Finally, over the long term, Serbia-Montenegro also faces the same problems as Croatia in building state and societal capacity for democratic civil–military relations. These include developing transparency and oversight of defence policy and the defence budget, developing civilian expertise in defence issues, and engaging civil society groups in matters of defence and security.

Institutional changes

As in Croatia, confusion in Serbia-Montenegro's constitutional framework has been a key obstacle to the implementation and consolidation of new institutional mechanisms and structures for democratic civil–military relations. In Serbia-Montenegro, however, this process has been complicated by the uncertain future of the Yugoslav federation itself, and the fact that the JNA/VJ was always an explicitly federal institution. From its beginnings, the FRY was a contested state. Kosovo achieved quasi-independence in 1999, eliminating the influence of the government in Belgrade and expelling the VJ. Montenegro has in practice been politically and economically autonomous from Belgrade since the late 1990s, and much of the population remains in favour of full independence. The VJ/VSCG retains only a small presence in the republic, which has its own armed force in the shape of its militarised republican MUP.[46] The army is funded almost entirely from taxes collected within the Republic of Serbia.[47]

As a consequence of this constitutional ambiguity, the introduction of new defence legislation in Serbia-Montenegro has proceeded slowly, and resulted in continuing uncertainty over the detail of arrangements for civil–military relations. For example, supreme command over the army continues to be exercised by the VSO – a Milosevic-era creation that leaves the division of responsibility and authority between its three members deliberately unclear. This has caused several problems. For example, under the tenure of President Vojislav Kostunica (president of the FRY until March 2003), the Council met infrequently and irregularly, and both Milo Djukanovic (President of Montenegro until November 2002) and Milan Milutinovic (President of Serbia until October 2002) were reluctant to take up their seats.[48] Moreover, even when the VSO did meet, under Kostunica it was reluctant to take tough decisions in the absence of consensus amongst the three presidents. This meant that, in practice, control of the army lay in the hands of the federal president alone, who in the event of stalemate or inertia within the VSO was able to use his powers of presidential decree to force through decisions. While this situation in many respects simplified the chain of command over the VJ, it also meant that the president was forced to exercise his control over the army in a constitutional and legal grey area.

No serious attempt was made to reform the VSO between 2000 and 2002. For the most part, this was because the government was reluctant to invest time and energy in reforming existing arrangements only to see these change again with the finalisation of a new constitutional relationship between Serbia and Montenegro.[49] This reluctance to embark on the development of new legislation was particularly acute in relation to the Yugoslav defence sector, because the army was by far the largest and most significant federal institution in the FRY, and so its reforms were closely bound up with those of the new state. Moreover, the sheer volume of legislative change that Serbia-Montenegro has had to attempt since October 2000, in all areas of the state, economy and society, has placed enormous pressure on already-limited parliamentary time and resources.[50] Until the introduction of the new constitutional Charter in 2003, only one major piece of defence and security legislation was passed by the federal parliament – the Law on the Security Services of the Federal Republic of Yugoslavia of July 2002, which was criticised for being rushed and containing major flaws.[51]

For most of 2000–03, there has been a continuing need to introduce new legislation that will provide a clear and unambiguous basis for developing democratic control of the armed forces.[52] The finalisation of the new constitutional Charter and the creation of the State Union of Serbia and Montenegro may at last provide the opportunity for the state government and parliament to address this deficiency. Even so, the new constitution is not without its problems and ambiguities. For example, it retains the VSO, but explicitly states that it can only make its decisions through consensus.[53] This removes the federal president's dominance over the command of the VSCG, but further complicates the chain of command and leaves open the question of how the army will be commanded in the event of a disagreement between the VSO's three members. In addition – and in common with the 1992 constitution – the new document leaves the role of the defence minister and the nature of his relationship with the VSO and General Staff in the chain of command unclear.[54]

The introduction of legal and institutional mechanisms for civilian control over armed forces is no guarantee of their effectiveness in practice. Throughout 2000–02, for example, then VJ Chief of General

Staff, General Nebojsa Pavkovic often acted in a manner which questioned the extent to which he considered himself beholden to the commands of his civilian masters, whatever the formal constitutional constraints on his position. Moreover, the effectiveness of institutional mechanisms for civilian control relies not only on the subordination of the military to the civil sector, but also on the ability of the armed forces' leadership to exercise internal control within the military itself. The issue of internal control within the VJ was highlighted when figures connected to the army were implicated in the illegal export of arms to Iraq in October 2002. This apparently occurred without the knowledge of the government or even the VJ leadership, leading some to question the extent to which the VJ as a whole – rather than just its main elements – was really under civilian control.[55] In the wake of the scandal, and public expressions of concern by the US and UK, the government dismissed two generals and established a committee to investigate the affair and prepare new regulations on arms trading.[56]

Despite these problems, the introduction of the new constitution does finally provide a more predictable legislative background against which further civil–military reform can take place. Indeed, and despite the potential problems inherent in the VSO system, on present evidence the new arrangement appears to work well. The VSO has met frequently since the assassination of Djindjic, and has proved itself both able and prepared to take tough decisions. These include the dismissal of the controversial head of the Army Intelligence Service, General Aco Tomic, on 21 March 2003 and the retirement of 16 high-ranking military officers linked to the Milosevic regime on 7 August 2003.[57]. How far this positive situation is ultimately sustainable will depend on the long-term workability of the State Union of Serbia and Montenegro, and on the commitment and approach of the real centre of political power in Belgrade, the Democratic Party (DS) led by Djindjic's successor as Serbian Prime Minister, Zoran Zivkovic.[58]

Depoliticisation and civilian control

For most of 2000–03, civil–military relations in Serbia-Montenegro were dominated by political divisions and rivalries within the DOS coalition and questions over the role of the army and its leadership in these civilian struggles. From the moment it came to power, the DOS was a disparate and divided organisation. It was made up of a number of competing political parties and personalities, united primarily by their opposition to the Milosevic regime rather than around any common political programme. At its most basic, this division focused around two main parties and two personalities: ex-federal President Kostunica and his conservative nationalist Democratic Party of Serbia (DSS) and, until his assassination in March 2003, Serbian Prime Minister Djindjic and his more reform-minded DS.[59]

The divisions in the DOS had an important influence on the way in which the government approached civil–military reform between 2000 and 2003. In particular, clear spheres of influence within the Serbia-Montenegrin security sector emerged between Kostunica and Djindjic, with the former finding a power-base in the army, and the latter looking to the republican MUP.[60] In one sense, this division of power and influence was a natural consequence of the FRY's constitutional division of power, in that Kostunica as federal president was de facto Commander-in-Chief of the army, while Djindjic as Serbian prime minister wielded ultimate command over the Serbian MUP. However, many observers in Belgrade believe that these apparent alliances had wider implications. They suggest that they date back to agreements between Kostunica and the VJ and between Djindjic and the MUP, that neither the army, police or any of their special units would intervene against the DOS-sponsored anti-Milosevic demonstrations of October 2000, in return for a 'soft' approach to military and police reform (and particularly personnel reform) by the new government.[61] Whatever the truth of this speculation, it is clear that, for much of the period between October 2000 and late June 2002, Kostunica was hesitant to push through key reforms in the VJ, particularly around the issue of Milosevic appointees in its top leadership. This was especially apparent with regard to the VJ's controversial Chief of General Staff, General Nebojsa Pavkovic.

Pavkovic was a Milosevic appointee to the Chief of General Staff position and a Milosevic loyalist. He had previously been commander of the VJ's Third Army, which was responsible for the army's actions in Kosovo in 1999, and which associated him with ethnic cleansing and war crimes. Moreover, the extent to which Pavkovic was willing to submit himself and the VJ to full civilian control was open to question. Throughout 2000–02, he regularly commented on key issues of Yugoslav politics – such as cooperation with the ICTY – in an open and partisan manner, and he was implicated in the resignation of federal Defence Minister Slobodan Krapovic in January 2002.[62] He also engaged in a bitter and public dispute with former Chief of General Staff and Serbian Deputy Prime Minister Momcilo Perisic, which culminated in the latter's arrest by the military counter-intelligence services (KOS) on a charge of spying in March 2002.[63]

Pavkovic's continuation in the crucial job of VJ Chief of General Staff was clearly problematic. Indeed, NATO countries had made it clear that they would not do business with the VJ while he was still in place, a stance which had direct ramifications for the FRY's prospects of joining the PfP.[64] Moreover, Pavkovic's willingness to criticise the policies of the civilian government clearly undermined the government's attempts to place the army under full civilian control. As a consequence, from October 2000 onwards, domestic and international pressure built on Kostunica to dismiss his Chief of General Staff. Despite this, Kostunica appears to have seen Pavkovic as an important, if unpredictable, ally at a time when the divisions in the DOS were consolidating, and it took nearly 18 months of growing domestic and international criticism for him to attempt to initiate the general's removal. However, even then, events surrounding Pavkovic's dismissal exposed serious problems in the FRY's civil–military relationships.

Kostunica's first attempt to oust Pavkovic through the VSO mechanism occurred directly after the Perisic affair in March 2002. However, this was thwarted after it came up against resistance from fellow VSO members Djukanovic and Milutinovic, who wanted to debate the issue further before any action was taken.[65] The VSO met again on 24 June 2002, and again refused to support the federal president unless he also removed other key personnel from the VJ leadership, including the chief of the military security services, and then Kostunica ally, General Aco Tomic. Kostunica rejected this and attempted to bypass the VSO and use a presidential decree to relieve Pavkovic of his duties and replace him with his deputy, General Branko Krga. Pavkovic declared the decision illegal and refused to go, but was left isolated after Kostunica obtained expressions of support from key generals. Pavkovic took his case to the constitutional court, but it was dismissed on 11 July 2002 on the grounds that the court was not competent to rule in such matters.[66]

The convoluted dismissal of Pavkovic highlighted three problems in Serbia-Montenegro's civil–military relations. First, it clearly illustrated important ambiguities surrounding the command of the army that were inherent in the VSO arrangement. In particular, the way in which the

Council could be paralysed by disagreement between its three members fundamentally questioned its utility as the key instrument of civilian control over the military. The 1992 constitutional provisions governing the VSO's operation were unclear as to where ultimate decision-making responsibility lay in the case of such a disagreement, and as a consequence provided the federal president with the opportunity to simply circumnavigate it through the use of his presidential decree. This in turn called into question the manner in which the federal president's control of the army could be held to account, and undermined the legitimacy and authority of any decision that had to be forced through in this way. Second, the affair showed the way in which deep political divisions in the civil sector were able to hamper the effective operation of mechanisms for democratic, civilian control over the military. Kostunica's opponents in the DOS had been calling for Pavkovic's dismissal for some time, but were prepared to jeopardise this through Djukanovic and Milutinovic's refusal to support him in the VSO. This had the short-term political advantage of damaging Kostunica, but in doing so it threatened to undermine the FRY's mechanisms for civilian control of the military.[67] Finally, Djukanovic and Milutinovic's stance in the VSO resulted from their perception that key elements of the VJ leadership were allied with the president. This in turn reinforced the arguments of those who suggested that the army had simply switched political allegiance after the fall of Milosevic, rather than attempted to embark on a process of depoliticisation. Moreover, Pavkovic's apparent willingness to defy the orders of the president suggest that, until June 2002 at least, civilian control over the army on the part of the administration had not been properly consolidated.

In addition to the events surrounding Pavkovic's dismissal, there were other indications of the VJ's politicisation, in particular that Kostunica attempted to use his close relationship with the VJ leadership to exploit the army for his own purposes. For example, some observers have suggested that the March 2002 arrest of General Perisic was ultimately inspired by Kostunica and partly a consequence of Perisic's close association with the Djindjic faction in the DOS.[68] In the wake of his dismissal, Pavkovic made public accusations – later supported by other senior VJ officers – that in June 2001 an intoxicated Kostunica had ordered him to use the army to seize control of the Serbian government's communications department because he believed that it was spying on him on behalf of Djindjic and the DS.[69]

Despite the chaos and political bitterness surrounding the affair, Pavkovic's dismissal may finally have laid real foundations for the full removal of the army from domestic politics. First and most importantly, it demonstrated that the VJ was ultimately willing to submit to the principle of civilian control. The dismissal of Pavkovic was a highly charged issue for the military, and one that Kostunica had been reticent about addressing for some time. However, despite Pavkovic's considerable efforts to protect his position, the army's leadership united behind the president and publicly declared their 'full readiness to ... implement all decisions taken by the Supreme Defence Council and the federal president'.[70] Second, the removal of Pavkovic eliminated a persistent and often vocal irritant from the Serbia-Montenegrin civil–military relationship. Pavkovic's replacement, Branko Krga, has been reluctant to comment publicly on questions of domestic policy beyond those which fall under his specific remit as Chief of General Staff.[71] Finally, while the question of the army's politicisation remains, the removal of Pavkovic lessened the potency of this issue by eliminating the personal connection between him and Kostunica and finally ending any deals that were made between the two in October 2000.

Events since the beginning of 2003 – not least Djindjic's assassination – have dramatically changed the political landscape in Serbia-Montenegro. Kostunica's own term as federal president came to an end with the establishment of the new state union in February 2003, and he has since become increasingly marginalised politically. Under the new constitution, the position of federal president is also less powerful than under the FRY, and Kostunica's successor, former Montenegrin parliamentary speaker Svetozar Marovic, is a less politically contentious figure than his predecessor. Taken together, these changes have removed many of the personalities and rivalries that contributed to the army's politicisation from 2000. They have also coincided with the introduction of the new constitution, with its revised provisions on the VSO, with the result that the VSCG's significance in questions of domestic politics, whether in its own right or at the behest of civilian politicians attempting to enlist it as an ally, seems likely to continue to decline in the future.

Transparency, oversight and expertise

For most of 2000–03, civil–military reform in Serbia-Montenegro has been dominated by fundamental challenges of institutional and legislative restructuring and the disengagement of the military from politics. However, the removal of Pavkovic in July 2002 and the finalisation of the new constitutional Charter in February 2003 indicate that these questions may for the first time be in the process of being resolved. In their wake, as in Croatia, longer-term questions of reform – issues of state capacity and institutional adaptation to the post-authoritarian political environment – are beginning to emerge as the most important concerns.

In both the SFRY and the FRY, the federal Ministry of Defence was largely a VJ institution. The majority of its personnel held VJ ranks, and in most questions it functioned as an administrative body separated from the Army General Staff, where the most important decisions related to the army were made. In the main, this situation has continued throughout 2000–03, though there are signs that this may now be changing as a result of the new momentum in the defence reform process. However, for democratic civilian control over the army to be consolidated in the long term, a degree of civilianisation of the defence bureaucracy, particularly of leadership positions, will be necessary. The 2003 constitutional Charter makes a start in this process in that it stipulates that the federal defence minister must be a civilian.[72] Beyond this, however, there has been no serious attempt to implement a civilianisation programme, primarily because of more pressing reform priorities elsewhere. In addition, the VJ's past dominance of the Ministry of Defence means that Serbia-Montenegro has no ready pool of civilians with defence expertise on which a civilianisation programme could draw. The Ministry of Defence's leadership remains sceptical about civilianisation because it sees little reason to replace what it views as qualified military staff with unqualified civilians.[73] These concerns reflect a wider institutional resistance within the army to what it perceives to be unnecessary outside interference in an area where it has always had control of its own affairs.

Current arrangements have helped to contribute to inertia in Serbia-Montenegro's military reform process. Both the army and the Ministry of Defence have been isolated from outside influences – domestic and international – since at least the beginning of the 1990s. Many observers suggest that its thinking on reform is inevitably characterised by passivity and conservatism, and that as presently constituted it does not have the capacity to deal with the challenges of reform in the post-Milosevic period.[74] In the long term, therefore, it seems likely that the Ministry of

Defence will have to undergo a more fundamental process of reform, including civilianisation, that will force it to confront many of the issues of institutional adaptation that have faced its Croatian counterpart.

Capacity problems have also been a significant obstacle to the ability of the federal parliament to provide oversight of the armed forces and defence policy. Under both Milosevic and in the SFRY, the federal parliament's input into defence matters was minimal, despite the fact that the VJ was by far the largest federal institution, and over which on paper at least it had significant powers of oversight. This lack of parliamentary engagement in defence issues has continued into the post-Milosevic period, with the majority of parliamentarians having little interest or expertise in military matters. Moreover, as in other areas of defence reform, uncertainty over the future of the federation and the future role of federal institutions led to a degree of inertia amongst parliamentarians towards their responsibilities.[75] In December 2001, for example, the federal parliament passed the federal defence budget, which comprised 4.6% of FRY's gross domestic product (GDP) and fully two-thirds of federal expenditure, after only two hours of discussion, and on the basis of a two-page document.[76] Moreover, a lack of defence expertise amongst many parliamentarians has meant that, even where they have attempted to tackle issues of defence reform – as with the 2002 Law on the [military] Security Services – this has resulted in poorly-drafted legislation.[77] As in Croatia, these problems have been intensified by a lack of resources for parliamentarians, such as library facilities, researchers and computers.

The period since February 2003 has been characterised by a more proactive approach by the government. A senior politician in the DS, Boris Tadic, was appointed to the position of defence minister for the new state. Soon afterwards, in March 2003, he presented a ten-point plan for defence reform in Serbia-Montenegro that explicitly recognised many of these challenges, and stressed the seriousness of the government's commitment to resolving them. For example, he emphasised the need to make the General Staff responsible to the Ministry of Defence and to 'relieve [it] of [those] duties ... not directly related to the main function, mission and tasks of the military'. He also prioritised the establishment of a modern defence planning and budgeting system for the Ministry of Defence, and the importance of strengthening parliamentary oversight in this area, calling for 'a radically different attitude of the military [towards] ... cooperation with the [new]

Assembly of the State Union of Serbia and Montenegro'.[78] This statement goes to the heart of many of the most important challenges facing the democratisation of civil–military relations in Serbia-Montenegro. Nonetheless, as the experiences of Croatia – and indeed much of the rest of Central and Eastern Europe – have illustrated, recognising these problems is only the first step in actually addressing them, particularly given the structural and attitudinal changes that this will inevitably entail. As a consequence, and whatever the government's good intentions in this area, it is likely that implementing and consolidating civil–military reform in Serbia-Montenegro will be a long-term task.[79]

Civil society

Despite its important role in other areas of politics, civil society engagement in defence and security matters was largely limited.[80] As in Croatia, this resulted from the tradition of exclusivity that the JNA/VJ had retained over defence issues in Yugoslav society. Since October 2000, this situation has changed significantly. A variety of Serbian-based non-governmental organisations now comment on and organise activities on defence reform issues. These include the Centre for Civil–Military Relations Belgrade (CCMR), the Helsinki Committee for Human Rights in Serbia, the G17 Institute and the Atlantic Club of Yugoslavia.[81] These organisations have engaged in a variety of activities aimed at promoting defence reform, including publishing analytical reports, organising workshops and meetings and running courses on civil–military relations and defence issues aimed at parliamentarians, policymakers, military personnel and journalists. While the quality and reach of these activities have been variable, they have sometimes also been influential. In November 2002, for example, CCMR organised a major televised conference on defence reform, bringing together representatives from the General Staff, the Ministry of Defence, the Foreign Ministry, the media and NGOs. CCMR also provides research staff for some federal parliamentarians.[82] The G17 Institute runs a School for Security Sector Reform, which aims to increase expertise on defence and security matters amongst civilian practitioners.[83]

In common with the Croatian experience, however, civil society's growing role in defence matters in Serbia-Montenegro should be qualified. At present, its activities are limited to a relatively small group of organisations and personalities based in Belgrade, and the extent to which these activities have genuinely influenced the defence reform process is difficult to assess. Moreover, most observers are united in their assessment that the media in Serbia-Montenegro continue to suffer from a severe shortage of qualified defence correspondents; partly as a consequence, levels of popular debate on defence matters remain low.

Chapter 2

Military Reform

The need for military reform has been a common feature across the post-Communist region, and indeed in Europe more widely. At the beginning of the 1990s, armed forces faced major challenges. Most had been organised and structured for Cold War missions and tasks, which focused around the defence of national territory in the event of a high-intensity European land war, and required large, generally conscript-based armed forces. The end of the Cold War fundamentally changed the strategic landscape in Europe, and with it the raison d'être of many armed forces. Across Europe, this led to a questioning of the military's traditional roles and budgetary allocations.[1]

Throughout the 1990s, the armed forces of Croatia and the FRY were largely isolated from these wider European trends by their involvement in the conflicts of the former Yugoslavia. Both retained traditional force structures, including a high proportion of conscript soldiers and a concentration on heavy armour and artillery, supported by high defence budgets. This isolation ended with the collapse of authoritarianism in 2000. The Croatian and Serbia-Montenegrin armed forces now face a vastly changed strategic environment, reduced defence budgets and the need to reform and restructure their force structures to meet the requirements of their new post-conflict, post-authoritarian circumstances. As in the rest of post-Communist Europe, this involves the related challenges of identifying the armed forces' new roles, and on this basis implementing military restructuring programmes and developing appropriate professional expertise.

Croatia, 2000–03

The Croatian defence sector was forged during the country's war for independence in 1991–95, and this legacy has influenced its organisation and structure ever since. In particular, it has had an important impact in three related areas which have come to dominate the practical implementation of Croatia's post-Tudjman defence reform process. The first is the large size of the OSRH, which at a strength of around 51,000 in 2002 is widely recognised to be disproportionate to the demands of Croatia's increasingly benign security environment.[2] The second is the composition of the officer corps at staff level, much of which is made up of personnel who achieved high rank through successes 'in the field', rather than through their suitability or qualifications for staff and command appointments. Finally, the size of the defence budget – which was sustained at over 8% of GDP between 1994 and 1998 – has made it difficult for reductions in defence spending to be absorbed without fundamental reforms in the way the armed forces are organised.[3]

The future shape of the OSRH is dictated by the National Security Strategy of 2002, which sees Croatia's military as a smaller, more professional force, able to participate in peace support operations in cooperation with NATO countries and to fulfil Croatia's obligations as part of the PfP. In February 2002, Defence Minister Rados announced the start of a plan that would reduce the active strength of the OSRH by 40% to 25,000; the Ministry of Defence by 2,000 personnel; and defence expenditure to 2% of GDP.[4] The ultimate future of conscription in Croatia is also open to question, and many officials wish to follow the plans announced by countries such as the Czech Republic, Hungary and Slovenia, and abolish it altogether. However, progress towards these goals has been limited, with no clear agreement as to how they will actually be implemented in practice.

Role

At the time of its formation, the role of the OSRH was clear: to defend the new Croatian state from the JNA and Serbian paramilitary organisations operating in Krajina and Slavonia. This imperative is defined clearly in the Croatian constitution, which states that 'The armed forces of the Republic of Croatia protect its sovereignty and independence and defend its territorial integrity'.[5] This developed during the war to include expeditionary tasks during its intervention in support of Croatian forces in Bosnia in 1991–95, and more offensive operations during the *Flash* and *Storm* campaigns in 1995. During the post-war Tudjman period, the OSRH's role continued to be seen largely in the context of territorial defence. The absence of any real effort to push through military reform meant that, in practice, the late 1990s saw the armed forces' progressive stagnation around its 1995 missions, tasks and force structures.

With the advent of the new government in 2000, the role of the OSRH came under serious scrutiny. The government plans a smaller, more flexible OSRH, still primarily focused on the defence of national territory, but also capable of contributing to multinational peace support operations and able to support other government departments in addressing internal security threats.

An important new role for the OSRH outlined in the National Security Strategy has been in relation to international cooperation and peace support operations. Croatia has contributed observers and specialist personnel to the UN operations in Sierra Leone (UNAMSIL, ten observers) and Ethiopia and Eritrea (UNMEE, five observers), made a 44-strong military police contribution to the International Security Force in Afghanistan in early 2003, and hosts the Regional Arms Control Verification and Implementation Assistance Centre for Southeastern Europe (RACVIAC) at Rakitje near Zagreb. Both the Ministry of Defence and Ministry of Foreign Affairs are vocal in their desire for Croatia to participate more fully in multinational operations and cooperative programmes.[6] Ministerial officials are explicit that this strategy is primarily driven by foreign policy, and is aimed at encouraging the closer integration of Croatian forces with their European (and especially NATO) counterparts. In this way, they hope they will follow the experience of other Central and Eastern European countries in showing public willingness to contribute to alliance responsibilities and commitments, and supporting the 'common values' of the institution concerned.[7]

Another shift in emphasis is the development of a role for the OSRH in the provision of military assistance at home.[8] This has focused particularly on the contribution that it can make to fighting the devastating forest fires that sweep the Adriatic region every summer[9]. While the Department for Rescue and Protection, which includes the Fire Service, was transferred from the Ministry of Defence to the Ministry of Interior in 1994, mechanisms for cooperation between the two ministries in this area remain strong. All fire-fighting air assets remain under the control of the Ministry of Defence for personnel and support reasons, and joint civil–military catastrophe planning and monitoring centres also come under the authority of its Communications and Information Technology Department.[10]

Restructuring

Successful restructuring of the OSRH is a fundamental part of Croatia's military reforms. This is particularly the case in relation to downsizing. A smaller, more professional OSRH will be better able to fulfil the roles that the National Security Strategy has prioritised for it. Some observers suggest that downsizing is the key to the whole future of the Croatian defence sector. At present, the OSRH is oversized and ageing, and its equipment increasingly outdated. The Croatian defence budget has been rapidly reduced since 2000, to levels of around 2.5% of GDP in 2002, and the effect of this has been to exacerbate the OSRH's existing problems. This combination of high manpower and declining resources meant that as much as 72% of the Croatian defence budget was devoted to personnel costs in 2002. Of the remainder, 20% was spent on the maintenance of infrastructure and equipment, allowing only 8% for everything else, including procurement.[11] The high proportion of defence spending absorbed by salary costs has come close to stimulating a crisis in the OSRH. Budgetary and personnel restraints have caused the government to freeze further (non-conscript) recruitment into the army. This has prevented the recruitment of the next generation of soldiers, and led to a situation where the average age of the non-conscript force is almost 38-years-old.[12]

To all intents and purposes, there has also been a suspension of equipment procurement and modernisation. The impact of this on the OSRH has been severe. Most of the army's existing equipment was second-hand when it was first acquired, either having been purchased from the downsizing former Communist armed forces of Central and Eastern Europe or obtained from the JNA in the early 1990s. In addition, it has been subjected to four years of demanding wartime usage, spare parts are generally unavailable and regular servicing and maintenance often do not take place. In 2002, the bulk of the OSRH's equipment was inoperative, unreliable and in desperate need of replacement.[13]

It is widely recognised within Croatia's defence community that addressing the OSRH's over-manning problem would unlock resources for selective updating of equipment, recruiting new soldiers and modernising the force. Certainly, at 2.5% of GDP Croatia's defence budget remains higher than the 2001 NATO average of 2.12%, and according to the assessments of outside analysts and the Ministry of Defence itself should be able to resource adequately a 25,000-strong OSRH.[14] Nonetheless, whatever the long-term gains of reducing the size of the army in Croatia, the short-term demands of such a policy make implementing it both politically risky and economically challenging. Indeed, despite various public pronouncements, the Croatian government has in practice attempted to side-step the issue. Where downsizing has occurred, it has generally been a result of the army's natural cycle of retirement coupled with the ban on new recruitment. Other policies in this area have sometimes been counter-productive, or have amounted to little more than tinkering at the edges. Thus, for example, the length of national service has been reduced from ten to six months, allowing smaller intakes of up to 6,000 recruits twice a year, and reducing the number of conscripts in the OSRH by around half. This measure has actually increased the frequency of the most resource-intensive phase of the conscription period – the first few weeks – while reducing the period in which conscripts are trained to such a low duration that their utility in almost all roles is highly questionable.[15]

If downsizing is to tackle the problems of the OSRH, it needs to take place amongst its volunteer soldiers on whom most of the defence budget's salary costs are concentrated. However, for this to occur the government has to overcome two serious problems. The first is socio-economic. Croatia's unemployment rate is high, at an estimated 21.7% of the population in 2002.[16] In this context, retiring, for example, 10,000 full-time soldiers from the OSRH may simply create 10,000 new unemployed people and shift resourcing problems into another sphere of governmental responsibility. While the OSRH's function as a social institution and a state-sponsored mechanism for providing employment is clearly not sustainable in the long term, it does mean that the short-term socio-economic costs of implementing a serious downsizing programme are likely to be significant.

A second and related obstacle concerns popular perceptions of the government's moral obligations to its soldiers, and their political ramifications. In Croatia, there remains enormous popular pride at the army's achievements during the 'Homeland War'. The OSRH defended the country against the initially overwhelming conventional superiority of the JNA and spent four years engaged in Croatia's often brutal struggle for national independence. The achievements and traumas of this period were exploited by the Tudjman regime in order to bolster its popular legitimacy. This reinforced the army's already-strong credentials as national saviour and foundation stone of the independent Croatian state. This central role in the Croatian national myth means that the government's treatment of its soldiers, many of whom are combat veterans, is a sensitive subject. In practical terms, this implies that any government (or minister) which implements a downsizing policy that is seen to treat the country's 'war heroes' poorly risks a serious political backlash. Moreover, there is also a strong and genuine sense of moral responsibility towards war veterans in the Ministry of Defence itself, and there is a reluctance to embark on policies which may result in making thousands of soldiers unemployed.[17]

These imperatives have been intensified by the continuing influence of the veterans' associations in Croatian politics and the renascent popularity of the HDZ. Both have placed the position of war veterans at the centre of their political platforms, and are fiercely opposed to any plans that threaten to leave former servicemen badly off. Their interest in veterans' issues means that any government policy in this area is subject to intense and often hostile public scrutiny.

These political problems are intensified by the demographic composition of the OSRH, another legacy of its formation in the turbulent early 1990s. At this time, most of the Croatian military's recruits were drawn from the more under-developed and nationalistic rural regions.[18] Today, these are the parts of Croatia with the highest unemployment levels, and where the HDZ continues to look for its core support. The implications of this for the current government are clear. If it implements a major process of downsizing, many of those soldiers it will forcibly retire will return to parts of the country where employment opportunities are the most limited. In doing so, they will increase the socio-economic strains on vulnerable regions, further alienate hostile constituencies and intensify popular support for the HDZ.

In order to help address these difficulties, the Ministry of Defence has attempted to develop a comprehensive resettlement strategy for those soldiers it plans to retire. The plan was developed in consultation with civilian experts, and recommends that soldiers are paid a proportion of their salary for a fixed period after their retirement in order to ease their transition into civilian life.[19] However, despite its undoubtedly forward-looking nature, the implementation of the plan remains open to question. The substantial costs have to be allocated from the existing defence budget, which means that it will only go a small way towards addressing the defence sector's financial difficulties. More broadly, there is little appetite within the Ministry of Defence for putting downsizing plans into action. There is, for example, no agreement on whether 'retirees' will be nominated by their commanding officers, or whether systematic criteria should be used. In relation to the second option, it has not been established what these criteria should be or who is responsible for setting them.[20] Moreover, since mid-2002, growing doubts have been expressed over the willingness of the government to invest the money saved by downsizing back into the defence sector given the other demands on the state budget.[21]

Expertise and professionalisation

As with so many other aspects of the OSRH, its structures for education and training have been heavily influenced by its formation during the war years of the early 1990s, and the approach of the Tudjman government towards the military more widely. The OSRH was established at a time of crisis, when recruitment of any sort was badly needed. As a result, recruitment criteria for soldiers and officers were haphazard, and often based on neither educational qualifications nor experience.[22] Promotion during the war was based on tactical experience and performance in the field rather than on education, training or other qualities.[23] Croatia's operational successes meant that many soldiers and officers were promoted, creating an oversized and top-heavy officer corps. Moreover, the politicisation of the OSRH by the Tudjman regime meant that both during and after the war, promotions often occurred on the basis of political loyalty to the HDZ or personal loyalty to senior party figures. Many senior OSRH officers do not have the expertise necessary for their peacetime jobs, which are often of a complex technical or managerial nature. Two-thirds of field officers (lieutenant to captain) have no college education, while education levels amongst middle-ranking officers – the majors and lieutenant-colonels who represent the OSRH's future leadership – are similarly limited.[24]

The Ministry of Defence has two issues to address in this area. The first concerns education and training for existing OSRH personnel. The second relates to the introduction of a new education and training structure for the armed forces as a whole. Croatia has no military academy, and the 'educational deficit' runs through the OSRH. There is no pool of expertise within the officer corps from which to draw instructors for any new initiatives. However, Croatia does have two options that may allow it to begin the process of 'training its trainers'. The first is the bilateral and multilateral military assistance programmes offered by Western countries and institutions. For example, US training assistance to the Croatian armed forces grew from $65,000 in 1995 to $500,000 in 2000 through the International Military Education and Training fund (IMET). IMET assistance has paid for Croatian military and civilian personnel to participate in training courses in the US, a series of one- and two-week seminars in Croatia itself, and the establishment of three language laboratories in the Croatian Military School of Foreign Languages.[25] Similar though less extensive education and training initiatives have been implemented by other countries, including Germany, the UK, France, Italy, Turkey, Hungary, Norway, Poland and Spain.[26] Second, the reactivation of Croatia's civilian defence studies courses since 2000 may offer the opportunity for the provision of military education through civilian universities. This is an option that both the Ministry of Defence and the University of Zagreb are keen to explore.[27] However, the civilian academics who would offer these courses complain that, despite much discussion, little has been done to implement this, and enthusiasm to do so appears to be waning.[28]

These difficulties in implementation are compounded by resourcing problems. Any changes in military education and training for the OSRH will have to be paid for from the already-straining defence budget, and will have to compete with the Ministry of Defence's spending requirements for salaries, pensions, procurement and maintenance. In real terms, therefore, the Ministry of Defence is faced with hard choices about its spending priorities. Western sources suggest that those Croatian students who have attended foreign courses are sometimes under-utilised or ignored, often because of the still-inadequate and clientalist human resource system within the military.[29] Moreover, the reluctance of the government to take tough decisions that will liberate the 'downsizing dividend' does not bode well for the future. On current evidence, it seems that military education and training will lose out in the political and budgetary struggle over the future of the OSRH.

Serbia-Montenegro, 2000–03

The JNA/VJ's experiences in the Yugoslav conflict and under the Milosevic regime have had a major impact on its development in the 1990s. In the main, these influences served to isolate the VJ from the common military reform agendas of much of the rest of post-Communist Europe, and stalled any real attempt at modernisation. As a consequence, the VSCG faces serious and pressing reform challenges. These relate to the evolution of its role and purpose in Serbia-Montenegro's new security environment, restructuring and re-equipping in line with this, and the challenge of professionalisation.

The future shape of the VSCG is currently under review. However, as with so much else in the defence sphere in Serbia-Montenegro, throughout much of 2000–03, modernisation and reform fell victim to inertia caused by uncertainties over the constitutional future of the FRY, and over the future position of General Pavkovic. Nonetheless, the direction of VJ/VSCG reform has begun to emerge. The army produced its Dynamic Plan for Restructuring and Reorganisation in October 2001, while the VSO announced a series of restructuring plans for the military in December 2001. In September 2002, the Defence Policy Department of the Ministry of Defence prepared a draft National Security Strategy with input from the General Staff. The publication of this document has been consistently delayed, but elements of it have emerged in statements by Chief of General Staff Krga and Defence Minster Tadic.[30] Broadly, these point to the goal of a smaller, more professional army, able to contribute to international peace support operations in the context of NATO's PfP, and better structured to support other government departments in addressing internal security threats.

Role

The role of the VJ was outlined in the 1992 constitution and refined in the Milosevic-era Defence Doctrine of August 2000. These documents are currently being superseded, with the introduction of the new constitution and the development of a new National Security Strategy. In the broadest terms, Article 133 of the 1992 constitution outlined the role of the VJ as 'to defend [the] sovereignty, territory, independence, and constitutional order' of the FRY.[31] In this respect, it continued to fulfil the traditional mission of defence of national territory (and federal integrity) outlined in the 1974 constitution. The 2000 Defence Doctrine confirmed this role, but included a new concentration on non-conventional forms of defence – a direct lesson from the Kosovo conflict – and re-emphasised the VJ's task of protecting the integrity of the federation, with explicit reference to the relationship between the Serbian and Montenegrin republics.[32] The 2003 constitutional Charter is less clear on these matters. As well as changing the name of the VJ to the VSCG, it defines its new role as 'to defend Serbia and Montenegro in line with the constitutional Charter and the principles of international law that regulate the utilisation of force'.[33] This rather vague definition is a result of the politically charged question of the position of the army in the new union. Montenegro retains a substantial constituency in favour of secession, many of whom view the army as an instrument of Serbian dominance. In this context, Montenegrin negotiators were reluctant to agree to any constitutional provision that obliged the VSCG to protect the integrity of the federation for fear that it could be used against them in the event of a bid for full independence. As a consequence, beyond the self-evident task of defending Serbia-Montenegro from external threat, the new Charter does little to illuminate the future role and purpose of the VSCG.

Despite this, statements by Krga and other senior officers from the General Staff indicate the direction of the army's thinking on the new National Security Strategy and the VSCG's developing roles. In particular, the army leadership has clearly recognised that the VSCG is in need of what Krga has called 'complete reform'.[34] In addition to the traditional role of the defence of national territory, the VSCG leadership prioritises the development of the army's capabilities in two areas. The first is its willingness and ability to contribute to international peace support operations. For example, at the end of 2002 Krga announced that the army was preparing a medical detachment of six personnel to be sent to the UN operation in the Democratic Republic of Congo.[35] More recently in August 2003, Prime Minister Zivkovic offered 1,000 peacekeeping troops in support of the US-led mission in Iraq while Foreign Minister Svilanovic raised the possibility of a VSCG contribution to the peacekeeping operation in Liberia. This emerging interest in participation in multinational operations is particularly instructive given the manner in which PfP membership has been prioritised in Serbia-Montenegrin political and military circles. This approach mirrors developments in Croatia and other NATO/PfP applicant states, where military participation in peace support operations has been used to indicate support for the Alliance's wider international security goals and commitments and showcase the abilities of the armed forces' best units.[36]

Second, the VSCG is prioritising internal security issues, particularly organised crime and terrorism. Indeed, since – and by some definitions including – the Kosovo conflict, the VJ's operational experience has all been in this area. For example, in combination with the Serbian MUP and in close cooperation with NATO and the Organisation for Security and Cooperation in Europe (OSCE), it played a key role in helping to manage an emergent ethnic Albanian secessionist rebellion in south Serbia in 2001.[37] This evolution in the army's role towards supporting other government departments in combating internal threats has been a common theme amongst the VJ/VSCG leadership. It reflects the FRY's own security preoccupations, as well as the implications of the 'war on terrorism' for the development of armed forces.[38] At the same time, the further development of an internal security role for the army remains potentially problematic in the longer term, particularly given the VJ's chequered history in this area during the Yugoslav conflict and current debates over the appropriate division of responsibilities in Serbia-Montenegro's already crowded security sector.[39]

Restructuring

Whatever roles the National Security Strategy eventually prioritises for the VSCG, it is clear that the army has a real need for fundamental reform and modernisation. In particular, its internal organisation remains structured around the demands of the war and pre-war years, including a large, conscript-based force structure with a concentration on armoured vehicles and artillery that is increasingly inappropriate to the army's evolving post-Milosevic roles. Moreover, much of the VSCG's existing equipment is ageing, obsolescent or was destroyed in combat, and will require (at least partial) replacement in the future. During the NATO bombing campaign of 1999, for example, some analysts estimate that the Yugoslav Air Force lost some 36% of its aircraft, including 11 of its 16 advanced MiG-29 fighters, while 60% of the country's air defence radar were destroyed.[40]

The fall of Milosevic created the political space for the VJ leadership to begin to think seriously about the need for military reform, and in October and December 2001 the VJ and the VSO announced a series of programmes aimed at restructuring the army. These included a plan to sell off some of the VJ's substantial real-estate holdings; a change in the army's configuration that would concentrate land forces into six corps and disband three army-level HQs, one divisional-level HQ and a number of units; a plan to integrate the air force, air defence and navy commands into a unified General Staff and to transform the air force, air defence and the navy each into a corps; a reduction in the size of the army to around 75,000 by 2003, with a further reduction to 60,000 by 2005, including the retirement of around 4,000 officers and NCOs; and a reduction in the conscription period from 12 to nine months.[41] However, these plans have come under considerable criticism from many observers, who argue that they reflect the army's underlying reluctance to address seriously the wider implications of reform. Critics also note that, until his dismissal in July 2002, Chief of General Staff Pavkovic was too preoccupied with protecting his own position to devote sufficient energy to the plan, and that implementation of its more substantive elements – such as downsizing the officer corps – was stalled as a result.[42] Critics suggest that the restructuring of the command structure is largely superficial, and has simply removed those parts of the army that had already atrophied, while the decision to reduce the length of conscription was taken for short-term economic reasons and was not tied to any broader vision of the practical requirements of the VSCG's future roles. Even since Pavkovic's departure, the extent to which proposed military reforms and modernisation plans have actually been put into practice, rather than simply talked about, is open to question.[43]

More widely, as in Croatia, Serbia-Montenegro's military reform plans have to take place against the background of major cuts in the defence budget. For example, between 1996 and 2000, Yugoslav defence spending under Milosevic was sustained at over 8% of GDP.[44] In contrast, the defence budget for 2001 was 4.6% of GDP, and looks set to fall even further in coming years as spending priorities shift from defence to other areas of political and economic restructuring. The impact of this on the army has already been significant. In September 2002, for example, the VJ claimed that it had already spent 98% of its budget for the 2002 fiscal year, and announced that it would have to send around a quarter of its soldiers home every weekend to save on food rations.[45] These budgetary constraints sharpen the need for rapid restructuring in order that the army can live within its means, and conversely indicate that extensive modernisation or reform may be financially difficult. In relation to procurement, for example, there appears to be a tacit acceptance in the army leadership that the steps necessary to re-equip some parts of its force structure – such as purchasing new aircraft – are simply too expensive.[46]

Despite these problems, many in Belgrade argue that there may have been a genuine shift in VJ/VSCG thinking on reform. They suggest that this has comprised a realisation that the current situation is unsustainable and that change must occur if the VSCG is to fulfil the demands of its emerging new roles.[47] Krga has made several public statements about the need for root-and-branch reform, while military reform questions and potential accession to PfP have become the overriding preoccupations of the Yugoslav defence community.[48] The beginnings of a new procurement strategy also appear to be emerging. This focuses on the introduction of new small arms (significantly in accordance with NATO standards), new ballistic protection and uniforms for soldiers, and modernisation of existing armoured vehicles. Current plans have focused these efforts on key cadres within the army, including special forces, military police, engineers and nuclear, biological and chemical (NBC) defence units.[49] This is important in that these are the parts of the army that are best suited both to participation in multinational operations and (in the case of the first two at least), for the internal security role.

How deep this attitudinal change in the VSCG goes, and the extent to which it will or can lead to practical reform, remains open to question. Certainly, if it is to be successful, it will require an effective analysis of available defence policy options, a realistic assessment of the relationship between these options and the resources available, and bureaucratic structures that are willing and able to implement policy choices. It is far from clear that the General Staff and Ministry of Defence in their present form have the capacity to meet these requirements. A clearer picture is likely to emerge once the new National Security Strategy and subsequent documents such as the new military doctrine are completed. Nonetheless, many suspect that the army as currently constituted is limited by what Miroslav Hadzic has criticised as 'a history of outdated thinking and a lack of practical knowledge', and that as a result it cannot easily be reformed from within.[50] If this is the case, addressing the military reform demands of the VSCG in the long term will require a much wider change in the way that the defence sector is managed and organised, including ending the army's institutional monopoly in this area.

Defence Minster Tadic's March 2003 statement on defence reform suggests that a new and genuine impetus for change may be emerging since the finalisation of the constitutional Charter – and, crucially, that it is civilian-driven. Certainly, Tadic has prioritised a number of key military reform elements as part of his ten-point defence-reform plan to 2010. These include finalising the National Security Strategy and the Defence Strategy and Military Strategy that would flow from it, and the need to introduce a new system of 'modern military organisation into the military that is in tune with the needs of Serbia-Montenegro and the requirements of the security environment we wish to integrate with'. While the statement is understandably short on specifics, it is noticeable that it is framed very much in the context of Serbia-Montenegro's desire to join PfP, and eventually to accede to NATO and the EU.[51] This suggests that defence reform has begun to acquire a strong foreign policy motivation. As in Croatia, this may in turn help to stimulate government interest in this area and provide a strong enough motivation for the defence sector as a whole to begin to address seriously some of its longer-term attitudinal and structural problems.

Expertise and professionalisation

In contrast to the OSRH, the VSCG is an established armed force whose history and traditions stretch back through the VJ and the JNA to the Second World War and beyond. The JNA and even the VJ were perceived by many Western military observers to be the most professional of all the armed forces in the post-Communist region, in the sense of having the appropriate organisation, expertise and competence to fulfil its roles. The institutional professionalism of the JNA/VJ is one reason why Milosevic took so long to establish his full personal control over it.[52] In this sense, the VSCG is not subject to the same kind of professionalisation imperatives that are so prominent in Croatia. For example, it has a well-established military education system, including a military academy that provides officer training as well as opportunities for postgraduate study and command and staff training.[53] Moreover, unlike the OSRH, the VSCG's human resource management systems did not have to develop under crisis circumstances, and its officer corps has long experience of fulfilling command and staff-level roles. In this respect, the VSCG does not suffer from an 'expertise deficit' to anything like the same degree as its Croatian counterpart. Nevertheless, the VSCG faces important challenges. In particular, the professional traditions of the old JNA have been undermined in three ways since the disintegration of the SFRY. First, the JNA/VJ was a key participant in the Yugoslav conflict. While many of the worst atrocities of this period were carried out by militarised structures other than the JNA/VJ, the army cannot evade all responsibility for war crimes and a number of former VJ personnel have been indicted by the ICTY. The VSCG's continuing failure to fully acknowledge these legacies is a persistent obstacle to its development of those elements of professionalism that embrace ethics and responsibility.[54] Second, the military performance of the JNA/VJ was poor during the conflicts in Slovenia and Croatia. While the impact of this was lessened – in the eyes of many Serbs at least – by the VJ's drawn-out resistance to NATO's 1999 bombing campaign, it did damage the army's reputation for professional competence. Finally, the politically-inspired purges of the JNA/VJ officer corps in the 1990s undermined the army's professional autonomy and politicised its appointments to command positions.

Addressing these issues will be a long-term process, and will require changes in the way that the VSCG is both organised and educated. These will have to reflect democratic and professional norms and values, rather than those of the Milosevic or SFRY periods. The dismissal of Pavkovic and the army's willingness to start thinking seriously about military reform may be the first steps in this process. Tadic's ten-point plan makes explicit reference to key elements of this professionalisation process, including the development of a new human resource management system for the VSCG, an increase in the proportion of all-volunteer soldiers and a far-reaching modernisation of the VSCG's military education system.[55] If these initiatives are to be successful, they will require a much wider attitudinal and behavioural change on the part of the VSCG than is presently the case, and a far greater willingness to acknowledge the implications of its past actions.

Chapter 3

The International Community

The role of the international community is important in any consideration of defence reform in Croatia and Serbia-Montenegro. In both countries, the legacies of the Yugoslav conflict, the development of Southeastern European defence assistance activities amongst Euro-Atlantic countries and the identification of membership of European institutions as key foreign policy objectives have given defence issues a special place in their external relationships and foreign policies. The prospect of NATO, EU and PfP membership, as well as the demands of cooperation with the ICTY, have been fundamental in both cases, and in all these areas the future of the defence sector is central.

From the perspective of Western countries and their institutions, promoting defence reform in Southeastern Europe is an important element of their wider policies aimed at encouraging democratisation and regional stabilisation. NATO in particular has been extremely active in relation to post-Communist Europe as a whole, and its activities in Croatia and Serbia-Montenegro build on these existing initiatives. Thus, for example, NATO's 1995 Study on Enlargement talks of one of the benefits of enlargement as being to 'contribute to enhanced security and stability for all countries in the Euro-Atlantic area by ... encouraging and supporting democratic reforms, including civilian and democratic control over the military'.[1] Similarly, Article 3 of the 1994 PfP Framework Document states that partner states will cooperate with NATO in facilitating 'transparency in national defence planning and budgeting processes', 'ensuring democratic control of defence forces' and developing 'forces that are better able to operate with those of the members of the North Atlantic Alliance'.[2] Specific programmes, such as Planning and Review Processes (PARPs) and

Membership Action Plans (MAPs) go further, establishing clear reform goals which partner countries are expected to achieve, as well as detailed evaluation procedures in order to assess progress.[3]

International influence in defence reform in Croatia and Serbia-Montenegro has broadly taken three forms. The first has been through defence assistance. This has consisted of bilateral and multilateral cooperative activities, primarily by Euro-Atlantic countries. The second has been exercised through pre-conditionality. This has taken the form of meeting the membership criteria of – again primarily Euro-Atlantic – international organisations. Finally, the international community has occasionally used direct conditionality. This has taken the form of threats to withdraw incentives or inflict punitive measures should either state not implement particular policies or obligations. Direct conditionality differs from pre-conditionality in that it is not a process which the target state opts into, but one that is imposed upon it.

Croatia, 2000–03
Defence Assistance

External defence assistance to Croatia has been substantial, and dates back to before the election of the new government in 2000. During the Tudjman era, the US in particular was heavily engaged in Croatian defence reform efforts. Initially, this assistance was indirect, through the activities of the private military company MPRI. While not an official arm of the US government, MPRI staff are drawn primarily from the ranks of retired US military personnel, and the company enjoyed official State Department support and approval in its Croatian activities. MPRI's official licence was granted on the basis that there would be no tactical component to its training, and that it would not violate the 1991 UN arms embargo on Croatia, which made direct military assistance illegal. MPRI's work with Croatia consisted of a series of programmes from 1994 aimed at encouraging democratic transition in the area of defence.[4]

Sponsoring a private company to carry out these activities provided an opportunity for the US government to indirectly engage with Croatia at a time when the undemocratic nature of the Tudjman regime made it difficult to do so overtly. This bolstered the United States' implicit support for Croatia in the face of what was seen to be the aggressive and regionally destabilising activities of Milosevic's Yugoslavia.[5] Nonetheless, serious concerns were raised about the suitability of using a company such as MPRI for these tasks. In particular, critics suggested that the successes of the OSRH in 1995 were a direct consequence of covert MPRI training and belied the terms of its US government licence.[6] Many have also questioned the suitability of providing former military officers as the primary conduit for assistance on issues of democratisation in the authoritarian context of Tudjman-era Croatia, as well as the democratic accountability and transparency of MPRI itself, and the quality of its training programme.[7]

Today, MPRI's engagement in Croatia is much more limited. It was supplanted from 1995 onwards by more direct military assistance programmes from the US and, especially after the death of Tudjman, by the development of more substantial efforts from others. Military assistance to Croatia through the US IMET programme has expanded considerably since the mid-1990s. In common with the defence diplomacy of countries such as the UK and Germany, this was initially aimed at helping to institute specific reforms with the objective of establishing democratic control over the OSRH, and preparing the ground for its application to PfP. Broadly, these programmes have included activities such as joint military exercises with Croatian forces, placing Croatian military students on language and military education courses in Western Europe and North America, running seminars in Croatia on issues such as the democratic control of armed forces, meeting Croatia's responsibilities under the Dayton Accords in Bosnia and the military and the media, and providing professional consultants to work with the Croatian authorities on key issues of defence reform.[8]

Croatia's relationship with NATO has also provided opportunities for defence assistance and cooperation at a multilateral level. This has occurred largely under the auspices of PfP (which Croatia joined in May 2000), and through its more explicitly targeted PARP, Individual Partnership Programme (IPP) and the MAP (which Croatia joined in 2001). Through PfP, PARP, the IPP and the MAP, Croatia has engaged in a variety of cooperative activities aimed at meeting the criteria for eventual accession to NATO and encouraging further defence reforms. PARP, for example, encourages partner countries to critically evaluate their own defence needs, and supports them in developing their defence planning capabilities. Croatia's MAP functions as a PfP-sponsored framework within which defence reform can be targeted, planned and implemented. Key aims for 2002 included the development of specialist forces better able to contribute to Alliance tasks and cooperate with other NATO members. This has concentrated on areas in which NATO and Croatia believe the country can make a particular contribution, such as a military police platoon, engineering, demining, NBC and medical and helicopter units, as well as the development of an infantry battalion that can be deployed abroad.[9]

Cooperation between Croatia and NATO countries in relation to defence reform has thus been extensive. For Croatia, any and all assistance in this field is welcome. Nonetheless, officials in Zagreb have raised concerns about the nature of the assistance and advice that they have sometimes been offered, and the problem of duplication. Certainly, in the early days of Croatian engagement with Western countries (to begin with almost exclusively the United States), there was a tendency to present the American model of civil–military relations as the best or only way forward, an approach which was criticised for being insufficiently responsive to Croatia's specific national circumstances. This 'one model fits all' approach to defence assistance has become less prevalent since 2000, but there remains a danger that particular approaches are presented to Croatia as 'the answer' to its reform problems – rather than playing a facilitating role that will allow the Croatians to find and develop their own solutions to these questions.

The involvement of other countries and organisations apart from the US in defence assistance to Croatia has gone some way towards addressing these concerns, but in doing so it has raised new challenges. Thus, despite efforts to coordinate activities through monthly meetings of the NATO attachés' club in Zagreb, some duplication of defence assistance activity occurs. While Croatian officials observe that this is not necessarily a problem – in that it allows them to assess the experiences of different countries and make their own decisions on what is best for their own circumstances – some suggest that it has engendered 'advice fatigue' amongst elements of the defence reform community, particularly in relation to activities such as seminars on civil–military relations.[10] Others argue that there is a danger that certain kinds of activities – particularly workshops and expert meetings – tend to target the same group of (generally English-speaking) Croatians, and so limit their impact by 'preaching to the converted'.

A consistent theme amongst officials engaged in defence reform in Croatia is that certain types of assistance and cooperation are more useful than others. In particular, more vocational and practical activities

– such as English-language training for OSRH and Ministry of Defence personnel, or joint military exercises or activities – are seen to have an especially important role.[11] From the Croatian perspective, language training allows access to a wider range of educational material and information, as well as enabling a greater proportion of the defence sector to gain access to the other forms of assistance that are available. Cooperative military activities are seen to have an important practical impact by introducing a broad range of OSRH personnel to the practices and operating procedures of larger and more professional allies, as well as having an additional 'trickle down' effect in the armed forces as a whole.

However, while cooperative activities in the area of civil–military restructuring have been generally well received and successful in and of themselves, questions remain about their real impact given Croatia's lack of progress in key reform issues, such as downsizing. Similarly, despite the Ministry of Defence's successes in preparing an infantry battalion capable of participating in multinational operations beyond Croatian territory, doubts remain amongst some observers about Croatia's financial and logistical ability to physically deploy this in practice, and sustain it over time.[12] Given the structural problems of the OSRH as a whole, the concentration of reform efforts on small specialist units may also camouflage deeper and more urgent demands elsewhere, and lead to a distorted approach to reform in the armed forces more widely.

Pre-conditionality

While Croatia's successful application to join PfP has allowed increased external assistance, it has also provided a new and demanding framework in which reforms must take place. This framework functions as a *pre-conditionality* mechanism through which NATO and its member states have encouraged defence reform in Croatia by offering a set of goals that it must meet if it is to come closer to its objective of NATO membership. In the context of Croatia's post-2000 efforts towards closer integration with NATO and other European or Euro-Atlantic institutions, membership of PfP, PARP and the MAP have all functioned as intermediary pre-conditionality incentives or 'stepping-stones'. Pre-conditionality has thus been a central strategy through which external actors have promoted their reform priorities in Croatia.

There is little doubt that closer integration with NATO is a key foreign policy priority for the Croatian government. This stems from political and popular perceptions of the advantages that membership of the Alliance offers. In practical terms, full membership of NATO would bolster Croatian security by incorporating the country into the NATO security guarantee. However, the practical implications of this are perhaps less significant than its cultural symbolism and its potential role as a stepping-stone to EU membership at a later date. Since the collapse of the SFRY, Croatia has identified itself, culturally and politically, as part of the Western European mainstream, rather than part of Southeastern Europe. This differentiation from 'the Balkans' dates back to pre-Yugoslav days, when much of the country was under the suzerainty of the Austro-Hungarian empire rather than the Ottomans, and plays an important role in Croatia's post-independence national identity. In addition, it functions as a public relations strategy through which the government can portray the country as a historic component of Western European civilisation and a 'natural' candidate for membership of European institutions.[13]

Indeed, EU membership is identified by many in Zagreb policymaking circles as the real prize in Croatia's efforts towards closer integration in Europe, because it will offer real economic and political advantages for the country and represent a final break with its Communist and authoritarian past. In this context, Croatia's defence sector has, almost by accident, found itself at the vanguard of a series of processes and priorities whose implications are far wider than simple defence and security concerns. Because of this, the pre-conditionality imperatives of NATO accession are potentially powerful motivators for Croatian defence reform.

While the government has taken important steps since 2000, and these have occurred under the framework of the NATO accession process, how far they have resulted from the presence of specific pre-conditionality targets rather than other motivations is difficult to identify. Croatia was heavily engaged in defence cooperation with NATO countries during the Tudjman period, and the US drew up a Road Map to Partnership for Peace for the country in 1998.[14] However, defence reform under Tudjman moved slowly, despite the regime's declared aim of closer European integration. The political changes of 2000 dramatically changed the context in which pre-conditionality was utilised. The advent of the new government – apparently committed to democratisation and reform – created the political space for the removal of many of the more difficult sticking-points in closer cooperation, including democratisation, economic liberalisation and a more constructive engagement with the ICTY. Under these circumstances, the prospect of closer integration with European institutions became a real possibility in a way that was always unlikely while Tudjman and the HDZ remained in power.

Those who have been involved with Croatia's defence reform programme since 2000 are clear that pre-conditionality incentives have been centrally important in dictating the direction of particular reforms once the basic political commitment to change had been made. Thus, the Croatian Foreign Ministry justifies the development of a peace-support capability in the OSRH on the grounds that it demonstrates Croatia's desire to contribute to international peace and security in a concrete manner; second, that it is a capability that NATO values from its members; and finally, that it publicly illustrates the government's willingness to support the goals of the Alliance, even though it is not yet a member. These justifications meet Croatia's responsibilities under the PfP Framework Document, and are tailored to support its NATO accession bid more widely.[15] Significantly, these capabilities have only been developed since 2000, and have occurred explicitly under the auspices of Croatia's NATO integration process. Similarly, the government's efforts in civil–military reform and structures for democratic control over the armed forces have occurred against the background of the PfP's requirement for democratic control of defence forces. While problems and delays remain, the demands of the PfP framework have helped to concentrate minds on these challenges and accelerate change at a time when political attention might otherwise have been directed elsewhere.

Nonetheless, the use of pre-conditionality in Croatia is not without problems. From the Croatian side, there are three main concerns. First, suspicions persist that the decision on whether Croatia will get what is on offer – in this case NATO membership – may ultimately be made on wider political grounds than the goals and objectives of PfP, PARP and the MAP. This in turn has created a degree of uncertainty over the nature of NATO's pre-conditionality demands. On the one hand, some officials in Zagreb worry that NATO may be tempted to add new membership criteria or demands at subsequent stages of its enlargement process.[16] On the other hand, of course, a purely political decision on membership could mean that Croatia is eventually admitted to NATO however well or badly it has done in defence reform.

Second, many in Croatia suggest that the pre-conditionality process might be more effective in influencing the country's defence reforms if NATO's criteria for membership were clearer and more specific, rather than comprising potentially amorphous and ambiguous principles such as 'democratic control of defence forces'.[17]

Finally, and notwithstanding the government's pro-NATO stance, there is a persistent and continuing scepticism amongst some policy-makers and analysts in Croatia that NATO's pre-conditionality demands are unreasonable. For example, many – including the HDZ – suggest that, for strategic and political reasons, NATO needs Croatia more than Croatia needs NATO, and that the onus for bringing the country into the Alliance should lie more in Brussels than in Zagreb, particularly given the financial and political responsibilities NATO membership entails.[18] Similarly, while opinion polls show popular support for NATO accession to be as high as 75%, many suggest that this results as much from a lack of real knowledge about the demands of membership as it does from a desire to accede.[19] For example, policies to address some of NATO's more onerous pre-conditionality criteria, such as downsizing the armed forces in order to increase their effectiveness or transferring indicted war crimes suspects to The Hague, have met with widespread popular and political opposition, despite their centrality to Croatia's membership bid.

The Tudjman period illustrated that pre-conditionality is only likely to have an impact when the incentives it uses are recognised and prioritised in the country in question. This points to two obstacles in the way of pre-conditionality in Croatia today. The first is that its scope may ultimately be limited. In particular, its influence may not be great enough to encourage the fragile governing coalition to push through unpopular policies. Second, pre-conditionality is likely to be most effective while Croatia has a firmly pro-NATO government. Given the resurgent popularity of the HDZ in 2002–03, there is a strong likelihood that its political influence after the next elections in 2004/5 will be increased, or even that it may form the government. Under these circumstances, making and implementing hard decisions over pre-conditionality reform goals may become increasing problematic.

Finally, there is a danger that pre-conditionality encourages a focus on meeting specific targets, rather than a more holistic and comprehensive reform of the defence sector. Thus, for example, Croatia has concentrated its professionalisation efforts on specific cadres and units within the OSRH in order to address what it believes are NATO's requirements and preferences. However, in doing so it has largely papered over the deeper and more pressing need for reform in areas such as military education and human resource management. This risks developing limited showcase capabilities that in themselves add little to Croatia's ability to provide for its own national defence – short of preparing the way for potential NATO accession.

Direct conditionality

Since 2000, the explicit use of direct conditionality in relation to defence reform in Croatia has been limited. However, it has played a role in the country's evolving relationship with the ICTY. Croatian cooperation on war crimes is likely to be fundamental to the country's defence reform, and central to its prospects for NATO accession. The war crimes question goes to the heart of the post-conflict rehabilitation of the OSRH, and without adequately addressing this sensitive area, the depth of democratic and professional reform in the defence sector will be open to serious question. In practice, the vigour with which this agenda has been pursued differs between different NATO and European countries, but it remains of vital significance and it is unlikely that it can be skirted or ducked by the Croatian government. It also provides the most likely opportunity for the future use of direct conditionality by the West.

During the Tudjman period, Croatia adopted a law on cooperation with the ICTY, but in practice its often obstructionist policies in this area were a direct influence on its exclusion from institutions such as the World Trade Organisation, the Central European Free Trade Association (CEFTA), PfP and the EU's PHARE aid programme.[20] The 2000 elections signalled a new context for Croatia's relationship with the ICTY. In particular, the new government was keen to demonstrate a renewed commitment to cooperation and to its obligations under the Dayton peace agreement in Bosnia. At this time, it was clear to many in Croatia that a more constructive engagement with the ICTY and the international community more widely over the legacy of the Yugoslav conflict would help to enable Croatian entry into a number of international organisations, and smooth the ground for its wider integration efforts. This more cooperative stance was quick to bear fruit. Croatia joined the WTO in November 2000, the PfP in May 2000 and CEFTA in March 2003. It was also invited to open negotiations on a Stabilisation and Association Agreement (SAA) with the EU in May 2000.

Between January 2000 and late 2002, Croatia's relationship with the ICTY was characterised by cautious cooperation, informed by continuing hostility towards The Hague amongst veterans groups and the HDZ. The government transferred Mladen 'Tuta' Naletilic – a key ICTY indictee – to The Hague in March 2000, and reached an agreement with the tribunal that lower- and middle-ranking war crimes suspects would be tried in Croatia. However, in September 2002 the ICTY formally requested the arrest and transfer of 83-year-old Croatian general Janko Bobetko for his role in the killing of Serb civilians in the so-called Medak Pocket in 1993. Bobetko – the highest-ranking Croatian to be indicted by The Hague – refused to recognise the tribunal's demand. In doing so he was publicly supported by the Racan government, which declared that it would 'defend Bobetko from unjustified indictment by all legal, political and diplomatic means', and launched an appeal against the ruling at The Hague and in the Croatian constitutional court.[21] The move sparked a series of bruising encounters with the international community, and saw the imposition of direct conditionality for the first time since the Tudjman period.

Throughout September and October 2002, Croatia was subject to intense pressure from Western countries and institutions. The UK suspended ratification of Croatia's SAA with the EU, scheduled for November, while both NATO and the EU explicitly and formally warned the government that its actions had jeopardised its accession bids.[22] In response – and after the failure of its legal appeals in both the ICTY and at home – in late October the government backed down and agreed to arrest and transfer Bobetko. However, soon afterwards, the general was taken seriously ill and given a government assurance that he would not be transferred while hospitalised.[23] A medical team from The Hague ruled that Bobetko was indeed too ill to stand trial; he died three months later, in April 2003.[24]

Direct conditionality played a significant role in influencing Croatia during the Bobetko affair. Throughout late 2002, discussion in Croatian policy circles was dominated by the damage that the incident had done to the country's NATO and EU accession bids, and clearly this was an important element in the government's eventual climbdown.[25] In November, a more conciliatory approach was adopted over ICTY requests to interview other prominent Croatian war crimes suspects.[26]

Nonetheless, the ability of direct conditionality to influence attitudes in Croatia above and beyond specific issues or crisis-points remains open to question. After all, Bobekto ultimately remained in Croatia until his death, and future showdowns with the ICTY potentially loom over other sensitive war crimes suspects, such as General Ante Gotovina. Moreover, in November 2002 the effectiveness of the country's own arrangements to prosecute lower-level war crimes suspects was called into question when a judge acquitted eight suspects on the basis that there was no evidence against them – a verdict labelled a 'complete outrage' by an independent human rights group monitoring the trial.[27]

The negative impact of this verdict has perhaps been lessened by a Croatian court's successful prosecution of indicted war crimes suspect General Mirko Norac in March 2003.[28] However, events since 2002 suggest that domestic pressure – in this case the continuing influence of nationalism and nationalist groups in Croatian politics – can still play an important role in defining the nature of Croatian engagement with the international community, however severe the consequences of non-cooperation may be. Given the damage that the Bobetko incident in particular has done to the government, and the populist appeal of the HDZ's hard-line stance on the issue, it also illustrates that, while direct conditionality can certainly achieve results, its use is not without cost.

Serbia-Montenegro, 2000–03
Defence Assistance

Even after the fall of Milosevic, external defence assistance to Serbia-Montenegro and the VJ/VSCG has been much less extensive than with Croatia and the OSRH. NATO countries have been reticent about embracing full cooperation with the Serbia-Montenegrin defence sector because of continuing concerns over cooperation with the ICTY and, until the dismissal of Pavkovic in June 2002 at least, the extent to which civilian control over the army has been properly established. However, there are signs that NATO is gearing up for a more in-depth programme of defence assistance to the VSCG, in the event that Belgrade meets its main pre-conditionality and direct conditionality demands.

For example, in cooperation with the Belgrade-based Atlantic Council of Yugoslavia, NATO officials held a private meeting with representatives of the Serbia-Montenegrin defence sector – including figures from the highest level of the Ministry of Defence, Ministry of Foreign Affairs, VJ General Staff and federal presidency – in May 2002 to discuss 'cooperation and partnership between FRY and NATO'.[29] NATO gave a further signal of its intentions when Yugoslav Foreign Minister Goran Svilanovic and Chief of General Staff Krga visited NATO headquarters in Brussels in September 2002. This would have been unthinkable while Pavkovic remained in his post.

The British Embassy in Belgrade was designated the focal point for the coordination of NATO activities in Serbia-Montenegro in 2002, and the British Ministry of Defence has been increasingly active in developing a programme of defence assistance. For example, throughout 2002–03 it organised discussions and expert visits on reform issues with key elements of the Serbia-Montenegrin defence sector, and offered places to VJ/VSCG students on English-language, peacekeeping, arms control and other military education courses.[30] The UK has also been invited to provide a senior military advisor (at the rank of Major General) to defence minister Tadic.[31] NATO countries have also invested efforts in supporting Serbia-Montenegro's burgeoning defence-oriented civil society sector, providing funding assistance for activities such as conferences and seminars, website development and publications. This has contributed to the capacity of these organisations to develop their own activities, and has provided additional, often indirect, opportunities for Western countries to engage with and support defence reform with official defence sector actors. These activities are likely to expand significantly should Serbia-Montenegro finally be invited to join the PfP programme.[32] External non-governmental organisations have also begun to expand their assistance. In December 2001, for example, the Geneva Centre for the Democratic Control of Armed Forces (DCAF) and the East–West Institute (EWI) produced a 1,000-page joint report for Kostunica that included a series of recommendations for security sector reform.[33]

The impact of defence assistance in Serbia-Montenegro has necessarily been more limited than in Croatia, both because to date it has been smaller in scale, and because Belgrade has embraced integration with Western institutions in a more partial and tentative way. Indeed, between 2000 and 2002, Belgrade's reluctance to address defence reform questions seriously meant that, even where assistance did occur, its impact was questionable.[34] Nevertheless, those involved in the provision of defence assistance state that even small-scale activities have had an important influence in encouraging elements within the Serbia-Montenegrin defence sector to think more seriously and systematically about how they approach their own defence reform process.[35] Senior figures in the army, Ministry of Defence and government appear increasingly minded to cooperate with Western countries, an approach that is reflected in a developing enthusiasm towards joining the PfP.[36] Indeed, since the finalisation of the new constitutional Charter in February 2003, those directing Serbia-Montenegro's defence reform process have increasingly framed their statements on these issues explicitly in terms of their aim of joining the PfP and, eventually, NATO and the EU.[37]

Pre-conditionality

Yugoslavia under Milosevic was excluded from membership of major European institutions and engagement in their outreach programmes to other states in the post-Communist region. In the period since October 2000, Serbia-Montenegro has begun to emerge from this international isolation. In doing so, the prospect of closer integration with Western institutions – and with it the beginnings of a symbolic return to the Western European mainstream – has emerged as a real possibility, and a growing policy priority in Belgrade. This domestic political prioritisation of closer integration has been slower to emerge in Serbia-Montenegro than in Croatia, largely because of the political legacy of the Milosevic period, the country's pariah status during the Yugoslav conflict and the NATO bombing of 1999. Partly as a result of these influences, the DOS coalition that took power in 2000 retained strongly nationalist elements and a suspicion of Western motives and policies. This has contributed to a continuing reticence towards Western institutions and their conditionality demands. Indeed, it was only in April 2002 that the government finally announced Serbia-Montenegro's intention to join the PfP.[38] This is in contrast to Croatia, which was admitted to the programme in May 2000.

Despite this, Western integration for Serbia-Montenegro has become an increasingly important element of the government's foreign and defence policy since the beginning of 2002. After all, closer cooperation and formalised association with Western institutions potentially offers significant advantages. It would open the door to more extensive Western reform assistance, and would function as a clear illustration of progress in Serbia-Montenegro's post-Milosevic transition, and therefore help to attract badly-needed investment. In addition, and excluding Bosnia, all of Serbia-Montenegro's neighbours are either full NATO members, have been formally invited to accede to the Alliance, or are members of PfP. This has reinforced Serbia-Montenegro's perceptions of geostrategic isolation, and placed further pressure on the government to engage more seriously with the pre-conditionality demands of Western institutions, and with their outreach programmes. Indeed, this emerging agenda has contributed to some of the most important reforms that the country has implemented in this period. This has been particularly the case in relation to Serbia-Montenegro's potential membership of the PfP, though it has also played an important role in its application to join the Council of Europe and its attempts to negotiate an SAA with the EU.[39] The pre-conditionality requirements of each of these institutions have at their heart issues closely linked to defence reform. Broadly, these concern the consolidation of civilian control over the army, and especially full cooperation with the ICTY.

NATO has been clear that there are several non-negotiable steps that Serbia-Montenegro must take if it is serious about joining the PfP programme. These have included or continue to include: an end to the army's links with the VRS, including financial support; support for all aspects of the Dayton agreement, including ratification; personnel change within the army to remove figures closely associated with the Milosevic regime or implicated in war crimes; the withdrawal of the government's lawsuit against NATO with the International Court of Justice over its bombing campaign of 1999; and full cooperation with the ICTY and full compliance with UN Security Council Resolution 1244 on Kosovo.[40] Broadly, these also reflect the demands of the Council of Europe and the EU in the defence sphere. Since the beginning of 2002, Belgrade has taken steps in all of these areas. For example, at the beginning of March 2002 it ended all official financial aid to the Ministry of Defence of the Republika Srpska and the VRS, while in December the federal parliament ratified the Dayton peace accords.[41] Moreover, a dawning realisation that Pavkovic's continuation as Chief of General Staff would always be an insurmountable obstacle to PfP membership appears to have been a key contributory factor in

Kostunica's decision to instigate his removal between March and July 2002. Kostunica's first unsuccessful attempt to dismiss Pavkovic occurred during the 25 March meeting of the VSO, when membership of the PfP was first officially suggested.[42]

The Milosevic legacy in the army undoubtedly goes deeper than one senior officer, and a number of serving personnel are implicated in war crimes. However, Western officials engaged in the PfP process indicate that the removal of Pavkovic alone may have been a significant enough step to meet NATO's pre-conditionality criteria as they relate to personnel change and a commitment to developing democratic control of the armed forces.[43] Certainly, since mid-2002 public statements by Western officials regarding Serbia-Montenegro's PfP application have placed less emphasis on the pre-condition of bringing the army under civilian control, in contrast to their still-trenchant position on the ICTY.[44] Likewise, while there are certainly continuing concerns over the other PfP preconditions – including implementation of Dayton and the need for further army reform – it is likely that these will not be a significant enough barrier on their own to prevent a PfP invitation. Given that existing PfP members include authoritarian states such as Belarus, Turkmenistan and Uzbekistan, and in the light of the steps that Belgrade has taken in relation to PfP conditionality, the case for continuing to exclude Serbia-Montenegro from the programme on this basis alone is declining in force. In addition, as the experience of states such as Croatia has illustrated, once Serbia-Montenegro is a member of the PfP the programme itself will introduce new opportunities for closer cooperation and may provide one of the most effective ways for NATO to deepen its influence over the country's defence reform process.

Each of the pre-conditionality demands that Serbia-Montenegro has acted on has involved questions of great domestic political sensitivity. These have been intimately bound up with the excesses and crimes of the Milosevic period. In this context, it is perhaps unsurprising that Serbia-Montenegro's nationalist politicians have moved more slowly than Croatia in implementing NATO's pre-conditionality demands. Nevertheless, since 2002 the incentive of PfP has undoubtedly contributed to the government's willingness to push through difficult decisions, an approach which, as the events surrounding the dismissal of Pavkovic illustrate, has not been without political cost. Indeed, senior government officials have increasingly acknowledged that the scale of the benefits that PfP membership – and

Western integration more widely – potentially offer Serbia-Montenegro are such that they are worth some of the short-term costs of meeting conditionality.[45] This position also appears to be reflected amongst senior figures in the VSCG, who believe that the requirements of PfP and even eventual NATO membership would support the army's own defence reform agenda of developing a smaller, modernised and more professional force structure.[46]

However, whatever the attractions of potential membership of PfP and other Western institutions, and whatever progress has been made in the pre-conditionality demands outlined above, the issue of cooperation with the ICTY remains unresolved. Cooperation, and particularly the arrest and transfer of former VRS Chief of General Staff General Ratko Mladic, remains the most significant obstacle in the way of PfP membership for Serbia-Montenegro.[47] The pre-conditionality process alone has not been sufficiently persuasive to encourage compliance in this area. Indeed, as in Croatia, cooperation with the ICTY is the one issue connected to defence reform that has proved problematic enough for the international community to resort to the use of direct conditionality.

Direct conditionality

Defence reform in Serbia-Montenegro remains inextricably linked to the question of war crimes and cooperation with the ICTY. This goes to the heart of the question of the country's culpability for atrocities committed during the Yugoslav conflict and the ability of the post-Milosevic state to acknowledge responsibility for these actions where appropriate. In turn, this is fundamentally important to Serbia-Montenegro's attempts to move beyond the legacies of the Milosevic period, consolidate its process of democratisation and normalise relations with its neighbours. The war crimes legacy and the question of cooperation with the ICTY goes far beyond the confines of the VJ/VSCG and the defence reform process alone. It incorporates elements from across the political and security sectors of both Serbia-Montenegro and the Republika Srpska, including politicians, the police and the VRS.

Nonetheless, the issue of the tribunal remains of particular relevance to Serbia-Montenegro's defence reforms. The army itself was implicated in war crimes in the 1990s, and a number of former VJ personnel have been indicted by The Hague.[48] The VSCG's willingness to acknowledge this legacy and cooperate with the ICTY would be an important step in the transition to post-authoritarian norms of behaviour, and an absolute perquisite for its membership of PfP. Second, the army has in the past been accused of sheltering indicted war crimes suspects, including Mladic, with or without the knowledge of the civilian authorities, and in direct opposition to the country's obligations under international law.

The significance which the international community has placed on Serbia-Montenegro's cooperation with the ICTY is illustrated by the extent to which direct conditionality has been used to encourage compliance. Most famously, direct conditionality played a crucial part in the attempts of the US and other states to put pressure on the Serbia-Montenegrin authorities to arrest Slobodan Milosevic in March 2001, and then transfer him to The Hague.[49] Direct conditionality also played an important role in pushing the government into introducing new legislation on cooperation with the ICTY and issuing domestic arrest warrants for war crimes suspects, including former VJ Chief of General Staff General Dragoljub Ojdanic, in 2002. Indeed, on 31 March 2002 the US government suspended all financial aid to the FRY on the grounds that the government was stalling on its obligations to the ICTY. This led to a flurry of activity in Belgrade, with the federal parliament passing a law on cooperation with the Hague tribunal on 11 April; on 17 April, the government publicly called on 23 indicted war crimes suspects to hand themselves in.[50] Five indictees including Ojdanic did so within the government's deadline, and arrest warrants for the remaining 18 were issued on 7 May.[51] As a direct consequence of these moves, the US released $40 million in aid to the FRY on 21 May 2002.[52]

Despite these initially promising moves, the ICTY again raised concerns over the extent of Belgrade's cooperation at the beginning of 2003, particularly in relation to its willingness to make available key documents, and with regard to the transfer of Mladic. Indeed, in January 2003 the US ambassador-at-large for war crimes issues, Pierre-Richard Prosper, announced that the government had to arrest Mladic and other indicted war crimes suspects if it was to receive further US aid after 31 March 2003.[53] This deadline was later extended to 15 June 2003 in the wake of the Djindjic assassination and signs of an increasingly robust approach to war crimes suspects on the part of the Serbian government, and appears to have been the decisive factor in the decision to arrest Hague indictee former Major Veselin Sljivancanin on 12 June.[54] Shortly afterwards, on 16 June, US Secretary of State Colin Powell decided to certify Serbia-Montenegro for continued financial assistance, despite expressing continued concern over the fact that Mladic and Radovan Karadic remained at large.

The manner in which direct conditionality has been used in Serbia-Montenegro since October 2000 illustrates both its effectiveness and its limitations in influencing the direction of reform, and defence reform in particular. Direct conditionality has clearly been effective in pushing the Belgrade authorities into taking explicitly mandated steps, such as the transfer of Milosevic or the introduction of the new law on cooperation with the ICTY. On this basis, it may have a continuing utility in relation to specific conditionality demands, such as the arrest and transfer of Mladic. However, beyond this, for much of 2000–03 Serbia-Montenegro's wider approach to the ICTY has been characterised by delay and creative non-compliance.

This is an area in which direct conditionality has had less of an influence, for two main reasons. The first is that the war legacy remains a deeply contentious issue amongst Serbs, and there has not been anything like a national, popular or political catharsis.[55] As a consequence, the ICTY remains deeply unpopular in Serbia, and there is a widespread perception that the whole process is discriminatory and anti-Serb. For this to change, there will need to be a much longer-term attitudinal shift at all levels of Serbian society. This is essential for the future democratic development of the country, but it is difficult to impose through direct conditionality. Second, direct conditionality has been primarily applied against the civilian government. This assumes that these authorities have the uncontested ability to implement conditionality demands. However, for much of 2000–02, the extent to which the federal government has actually been able to exercise full control over the defence and security sector – the cooperation of which is central to the apprehension of war crimes suspects – has been open to question. Indeed, the fact that Pavkovic as well as other senior officers were implicated in war crimes meant that cooperation with the ICTY directly threatened important personal and institutional interests in the army itself. This has led many to suspect that the army has been protecting key ICTY indictees, or at the very least has been reluctant to move against them.[56] Moreover, while civilian control over the VJ/VSCG may have been significantly strengthened since the dismissal of Pavkovic and there are indications that it has abandoned its position of protecting ICTY indictees, the army as a whole remains hostile to any implication that it was engaged in war crimes in the 1990s.[57] As a consequence, it is likely to prove a recalcitrant partner in any further government attempt to implement ICTY demands.[58]

In addition, and as in Croatia, the use of direct conditionality against Serbia-Montenegro is not without cost. The domestic political context remains sympathetic to nationalism and hostile to The Hague, and there is a danger that pushing too hard on cooperation with the ICTY may damage the wider reform agenda and stimulate a nationalist backlash.[59] It is also clear that any decision to order the army to arrest Mladic – who remains in hiding and reportedly protected by well-armed paramilitaries – would test the extent of the government's control over the VSCG and is a step that the civilian authorities may be reluctant to take.[60] None of these dangers is an excuse for Serbia-Montenegro not to cooperate with the ICTY. This must happen if the country is to face up to its past and complete its post-authoritarian transition. Nevertheless, they do point to some of the more negative implications of using direct conditionality to try to force the issue, and suggest that this should be limited only to questions of real significance and in the context of a proper assessment of the costs and benefits of doing so.

Conclusion

Since 2000, and despite important differences in scale and context, Croatia and Serbia-Montenegro have shared a series of important defence reform challenges as part of their wider processes of post-conflict and post-authoritarian transition. Moreover, in both cases – and again despite some important national differences – the underlying defence reform agenda in both Croatia and Serbia-Montenegro has increasingly followed the pattern of post-authoritarian civil–military transition established elsewhere in post-Communist Europe in the 1990s.

In Central and Eastern Europe, institutional reforms which depoliticised the armed forces and placed them under civilian control have been followed by a much longer-term process aimed at consolidating the democratic nature of this control in relation to areas such as transparency, oversight, expertise, effectiveness and efficiency. Military reform questions have primarily concerned the need to identify new roles for the military in the context of a radically changed security and budgetary environment, and to develop appropriate new force structures on this basis. Across the post-Communist region, these have focused on establishing an appropriate balance between professionalised forces able to participate in (often NATO-led) multinational operations, and the need to provide for affordable defence of national territory. In all cases, the prospect of closer integration with Western institutions – and particularly NATO – has been of great importance, and has enabled these institutions to exert a significant influence over the direction of defence reform in these states. These common themes of post-Communist defence reform have been apparent in Croatia, and are increasingly emergent in Serbia-Montenegro.

The new governments of both countries have faced the task of placing the politicised armed forces of the former regimes under civilian control and democratising the nature of this control. In Croatia, there has been significant progress. In particular, legislation and procedures have been introduced that reinforce the principle of civilian control over the armed forces, and the Tudjman-era politicisation of the defence sector has declined significantly. There has also been progress in these areas in Serbia-Montenegro, though for a variety of reasons it has been slower than in Croatia. The principle of civilian control has been established and demonstrated, while an important symbolic and practical step towards the depoliticisation of the military leadership occurred with the dismissal of Pavkovic in July 2002. Given the legacies of both Croatia and Serbia-Montenegro's authoritarian and Communist pasts, the extent of the progress that both countries have made in these areas should not be underestimated.

Nonetheless, both countries still face serious and persistent problems in consolidating these arrangements. In Croatia, there is little doubt that civilian control over the OSRH is a reality, but the democratic quality of this control – in relation to the implementation of defence policy, transparency and accountability – remains open to question. Continuing tensions and rivalries between the government, president, parliament and general staff mean that Croatia's new institutional arrangements for democratic, civilian control of the armed forces are often unwieldy and conflictual. This has complicated the civil–military relationship, and at times has placed important defence policy questions – which in themselves are often politically uncontentious – at the mercy of domestic political squabbles and personal rivalries. These tensions extend into the institutions themselves. For example, inter-departmental relationships within the Ministry of Defence have often been characterised as much by competition as cooperation, with the result that the implementation of key defence policies has been prevented or delayed. In addition, while the influence of Tudjman-era HDZ politicisation in the upper echelons of the defence sector may have diminished, it is far from clear that clientalism and patronage have done the same. Finally, there is a deficit of civilian expertise on defence matters within the Ministry of Defence, the presidency and parliament, compounded by a political deprioritisation of defence issues in relation to other areas of state responsibility and public spending. This has made it more difficult for all actors to formulate, implement and scrutinise policy, with particularly negative implications for the effective exercise of parliamentary oversight.

In Serbia-Montenegro, the extent to which the VJ was actually under the control of the civilian authorities remained open to question between 2000 and 2002. For much of this period, the army's leadership, particularly Pavkovic, appeared to be semi-autonomous, able and prepared to comment on questions of domestic politics and operating merely in alliance with, rather than under the control of, key actors in the civil sector. While the dismissal of Pavkovic clearly changed the nature of the civil–military relationship and contributed to the consolidation of the principle of civilian control, the VSCG remains largely a closed institution with significant autonomy.

Nonetheless, this factor is unlikely to lead to a serious military challenge to civilian authority in Serbia-Montenegro and, since mid-2002, the VJ/VSCG leadership has been at pains to stay out of politics and concentrate on its own reform process. The dismissal of 16 senior officers by the VSO in August 2003 has also illustrated that civilian control over the post-Pavkovic VSCG is very much a reality. However, consolidating and democratising the nature of this control will involve overcoming long-established norms of military behaviour and autonomy, a process which is unlikely to occur overnight.

Beyond these core questions of civilian control over the VSCG, Serbia-Montenegro faces many of the same challenges as Croatia in democratising its civil–military relations. Chains of command over the army remain ambiguous and unclear, the Ministry of Defence remains a closed and military-dominated institution, parliament's role in providing oversight of the policymaking process is minimal, and civil society engagement in defence matters is limited.

There are signs that these challenges have begun to climb the political agenda in Belgrade. This has particularly been the case since the events of 2002 and the finalisation of the new constitutional Charter in February 2003, which have cleared the ground for a more serious approach to defence reform. However, the democratisation of civil–military relations in Serbia-Montenegro may ultimately be more dependent on the evolution and character of the domestic political environment rather than the strength or weakness of its mechanisms for civilian control of the armed forces. Indeed, several of the most serious civil–military problems of the 2000–03 period resulted primarily from the willingness of civilian politicians to exploit the support of the army (and the security sector more widely) in their own political and personal struggles and rivalries. In the absence of a wider democratic context to frame a system of civilian control over the armed forces, the democratic nature of this control is always likely to be open to question.

The events surrounding Djindjic's assassination also illustrate that defence reform is only one aspect of Serbia-Montenegro's post-authoritarian transition, and point to an important difference between Croatia and Serbia-Montenegro in this area. The obviously deep and criminal involvement of the JSO in domestic politics in Serbia-Montenegro highlights the problematic and persistent question of Milosevic's non-VSCG militarised formations, and suggests that, if the country is to succeed in its democratic transition, wider issues of security sector reform must also be urgently addressed.[1]

Croatia and Serbia-Montenegro also face common challenges in relation to the organisational reform of their armed forces. Since 2000, both have struggled to implement serious military reforms in an environment where the armed forces' new roles have been unclear or emergent and their budgets drastically cut. The collapse of authoritarianism in both states and the termination of the conflicts of the former Yugoslavia has radically changed their geopolitical and geostrategic position and priorities, with major implications for the role and structure of their armed forces. These changes have had a two-fold impact. The first has been a decline in the relevance and utility of large, conscript-based armed forces structured for the defence of national territory. The second is to do with economic constraints and changing political and social-spending priorities, which has created pressure to reduce previously high levels of defence spending.

Croatia has perhaps progressed the furthest in addressing these challenges. The new government identified NATO accession as a foreign policy priority early on, and this has helped to frame its thinking and resulted in a series of national security documents identifying the future roles of the OSRH and the goals of Croatian military reform. Broadly, these concern the continuation of its traditional mission of the defence of national territory – albeit in a more benign regional security environment – coupled with the development of capabilities that will allow Croatia to participate in (primarily NATO-led) multinational operations and an increased role for the OSRH in providing assistance in times of natural disaster. These roles require smaller, more professional armed forces able to be deployed and sustained in complex operations beyond national territory. Whatever the declared intentions of the Croatian government in relation to military reform, though, the economic and political demands of these changes are severe, and they have proved difficult to implement in practice. In particular, the question of downsizing remains pressing, as does the need to recruit a new generation of volunteer soldiers to replace the OSRH's aging force. If Croatia's defence reforms are to be a success in the longer term, they will also have to address the 'expertise gap' in the OSRH through the development of effective military education and training, particularly at staff level.

In Serbia-Montenegro, progress in military reform was stalled for much of 2000–03 by uncertainties over the future of Pavkovic and a lack of domestic political consensus on both the future of the Yugoslav federation and its foreign policy. While reforms were announced, they occurred largely in response to immediate economic pressures rather than from any proactive vision of the roles and requirements of the army. However, a more coherent approach to military reform does now appear to be emerging in Belgrade. This is characterised by the appointment of Boris Tadic to the post of defence minister; his first substantive step was to spell out an ambitious plan for defence reform.[2] This follows the government's decision to apply to join the PfP programme, and has been accompanied by the gradual elucidation of new roles for the army. These reflect Belgrade's current security preoccupations, and include the development of the VSCG's potential for participation in multinational operations, in line with the perceived requirements of the PfP, and a reemphasis on the army's role in supporting other government departments in combating internal security problems. Serbia-Montenegro is at the very beginning of this process, and as in Croatia, the economic and political demands of actually implementing reform are in practice likely to be high. To be successful, they will require a clear vision of what will be required in future, an understanding of the demands this will make in terms of equipment and human resources, and a realistic assessment of how this can be carried out within existing resource constraints. This in turn will require a serious commitment to the reform process on the part of both the military and civilian leadership.

As in Central and Eastern Europe more widely, the international community is likely to play an important role in defence reform in both

Croatia and Serbia-Montenegro. In Croatia, the pre-conditionality demands of the PfP, the PARP and the MAP have helped to place defence reform at the very heart of the country's bid for closer integration with Western institutions. NATO – with its various pre-accession programmes, plans and associations – has been a key influence in this area. Its accession criteria are less demanding than those of the EU, and as such it has been seen by many countries in the post-Communist region – Croatia included – as the best option for early membership of one of the key European institutions. Because of this, and because of NATO's focus on security issues, defence reform in Croatia has assumed a political significance beyond the national security sphere. It represents an important step towards reintegration with the rest of Europe, and is seen by many in Zagreb as an important stepping-stone towards eventual membership of the EU. By tying the key foreign policy goal of accession to issues of defence reform, NATO has been able to push these up the Croatian political agenda and provide an important motivation for the government to invest political capital in addressing them. In supporting this with its own defence assistance programmes, it has also been able to shape the direction of this reform.

In Serbia-Montenegro, closer integration with NATO has not acquired the same urgency and importance as it has in Croatia. There are signs that this may be beginning to change, and that both the civilian government and the military leadership increasingly see membership of the PfP and even eventually of NATO itself as important and desirable goals. Indeed, there is a growing recognition in Belgrade that meeting PfP and NATO's pre-conditionality demands would unlock significant defence assistance from Western countries and function as a public indication of the changes in the country since the fall of Milosevic. If this pro-integration agenda is sustained, it is likely that it will concentrate minds on defence reform questions and provide the motivation for investing political capital in some of its necessary but more difficult areas.

The experiences of both Croatia and Serbia-Montenegro since 2000 also illustrate that, despite the undoubtedly influential role that the international community might be able to play in prioritising and shaping the direction of defence reform, this should not be overstated. Indeed, in both cases the international community's ability to influence the foundational assumptions against which reform must take place has been limited. Croatia, for example, was subject to the PfP's pre-conditionality demands throughout much of the Tudjman period, yet it was only after the election of the new government in 2000 that these began to have an impact on the reform process. In Serbia-Montenegro, the prioritisation of PfP membership could not be imposed from outside, whatever its apparent 'objective' benefits, but was a position that the domestic political élite had to come to itself over a period of almost two years, against the background of historically-informed political and attitudinal obstacles. This suggests that local ownership of a reform process is of central importance if it is to be sustainable in the long term. This point is further reinforced by the consistent reluctance of Serbia-Montenegro, and to a lesser extent Croatia, to cooperate fully with the ICTY, despite intense pressure from outside, including the application of direct conditionality.

Defence reform is an important element of both Croatia's and Serbia-Montenegro's wider processes of post-conflict, post-authoritarian transition. However, it cannot occur in isolation from them, and is to a large degree dependent on them for its own success. These wider processes of change entail meeting the political, attitudinal and social legacies of the authoritarian and conflict periods, and necessarily take place over the long term. These changes can be encouraged by the international community, which, through defence assistance and the careful use of pre- and direct conditionality, can also influence their direction and character. However, for transition to be genuine and lasting, its impetus must ultimately come from within. This paper suggests that, in relation to defence reform at least, this internal impetus for change has emerged in Croatia, and is emergent in Serbia-Montenegro. Since 2000, the defence reform processes of both states have become increasingly concerned with the common challenges of post-Communist transition, and have become more normalised as a result. As a consequence, the post-conflict and post-authoritarian rehabilitation of both countries may be a more realistic prospect today than at any other point since the collapse of Yugoslavia in 1991.

Notes

The author would like to express his appreciation for the critical comments and support given by Alex Bellamy, Malcolm Chalmers, James Gow, Miroslav Hadzic (and all the staff at CCMR Belgrade), Zvonimir Mahecic, Angus Morris, Richard Thornely, Witek Nowosielski and Ozren Zunec at the research stage of this paper. The analysis, opinions and conclusions expressed or implied in this paper, however, remain the author's alone.

Introduction

[1] In February 2003, the Federal Republic of Yugoslavia (FRY) introduced a new constitutional Charter and became the confederative State Union of Serbia and Montenegro (SUSM). This paper addresses defence reform in FRY and SUSM including the republics of Serbia and Montenegro but excluding Kosovo, which, while still nominally part of Serbia, has its own very particular political circumstances. To reduce confusion over the changing nomenclature these developments have entailed, this paper uses the term Serbia-Montenegro to refer to both political entities, except in circumstances where greater specificity is required.

[2] See, for example, Andrew Cottey, Timothy Edmunds and Anthony Forster, 'The Second Generation Problematic', *Armed Forces and Society*, vol. 29, no. 1, Autumn 2002; Anthony Forster, Timothy Edmunds and Andrew Cottey, 'Introduction: The Professionalisation of Armed Forces in Postcommunist Europe', in Anthony Forster, Timothy Edmunds and Andrew Cottey (eds), *The Challenge of Military Reform in Postcommunist Europe: Building Professional Armed Forces* (Basingstoke: Palgrave, 2002); Timothy Edmunds, 'NATO, Defence Reform and the New Member States', *Survival*, Fall 2003.

[3] Alex J. Bellamy, '"Like Drunken Geese in the Fog": Developing Democratic Control of Armed Forces in Croatia', in Andrew

Cottey, Timothy Edmunds and Anthony Forster (eds), *Democratic Control of the Military in Postcommunist Europe: Guarding the Guards* (Basingstoke: Palgrave, 2002), p. 174.

4 This paper uses the term OSRH to refer to the regular armed forces of Croatia as a whole, including the Croatian Army (HV), and the small Croatian Navy (HRM) and Croatian Air Force (HRZ). Colloquially, the OSRH are often referred to simply as the 'HV', though this was phased out of official usage from around 1996.

5 Bellamy, '"Like Drunken Geese"', p. 176.

6 TO units were a feature of the defence system of the Socialist Federative Republic of Yugoslavia (SFRY). They emerged from the Yugoslav partisan tradition and consisted of locally commanded militias made up of reservists. For further details see James Gow, *Legitimacy and the Military: The Yugoslav Crisis* (London: Pinter Publishers, 1992) pp. 45–50.

7 Both *Flash* and *Storm* were accompanied by the mass exodus of large numbers of Serbian civilians from these territories.

8 See, for example, Laura Silber and Allan Little, *The Death of Yugoslavia* (London: Penguin, 1995), pp. 360–61.

9 Yugoslav practice has been to refer to the armed forces as a whole as the 'Yugoslav Army' or 'VJ'. In practice, the Yugoslav Navy (JRM) remains small and only semi-operational, while the Yugoslav Air Force (JRV) and Air Defence Command (PVO)

were severely damaged during the NATO bombings of 1999. All are now integrated into the unified command structure of the newly renamed army of Serbia and Montenegro (VSCG).

10 Gow, *Legitimacy and the Military*, p. 59.

11 James Gow, 'Professionalisation and the Yugoslav Army', in Anthony Forster, Timothy Edmunds and Andrew Cottey (eds), *The Challenge of Military Reform in Postcommunist Europe: Building Professional Armed Forces* (Basingstoke: Palgrave-Macmillan, 2002), p. 186.

12 Miroslav Hadzic, *The Yugoslav People's Agony: The Role of the Yugoslav People's Army* (Aldershot: Ashgate, 2002), p. 259.

13 For further discussion of the VJ's role in the war, see James Gow, *The Serbian Project and Its Adversaries: A Strategy of War Crimes* (London: Hurst and Company, 2003), pp. 75–89.

Chapter 1

1 Andrew Cottey, Timothy Edmunds and Anthony Forster, 'The Second Generation Problematic: Rethinking Democracy and Civil–Military Relations', *Armed Forces and Society*, vol. 29, no. 1, Autumn 2002.

2 'Security and Foreign Forces, Croatia', *Jane's Sentinel Security Assessment – The Balkans* – p. 10, 27 February 2002.

3 Ozren Zunec, 'Democracy in the "Fog of War": Civil–Military Relations in Croatia', in Constantine Danopoulos and Daniel Zirker (eds), *Civil–*

Military Relations in the Soviet and Yugoslav Successor States (Boulder, CO: Westview, 1996), p. 225; interview with General Pavao Miljavac, Parliamentary Committee for Internal Affairs and National Security, former Minister of Defence of the Republic of Croatia, Zagreb, 9 July 2002.

4 Zunec, 'Democracy in the "Fog of War", p. 225; Bellamy, '"Like Drunken Geese in the Fog"', p. 175; correspondence with Zunec, Professor of Sociology, Zagreb University, 15 April 2003.

5 Zoran Kusovac, 'HDZ Tests Croat Coalition', *Jane's Intelligence Review*, vol. 13, no. 4, 1 April 2001, pp. 20–21; correspondence with Zunec.

6 Vesna Pusic has called Tudjman's Croatia 'a dictatorship with democratic legitimacy'. See Vesna Pusic, 'Dictatorships with Democratic Legitimacy: Democracy Versus Nation', *East European Politics and Societies*, vol. 8, no. 4, 1994, p. 397.

7 Articles 80, 112, *Constitution of the Republic of Croatia*, 2000.

8 Articles 93, 99, *Constitution of the Republic of Croatia*.

9 Zvonimir Mahecic, 'Defence Reform and the Role of State Institutions: Croatian Experiences', *CMR Network*, no. 6, October 2002, p. 8.

10 Correspondence with Mahecic, 29 April 2003.

11 Articles 6, 7, 8, *Defence Law of the Republic of Croatia*, 2002.

12 Articles 7, 10, *Defence Law of the Republic of Croatia*, 2002.

13 Mahecic, 'Defence Reform', p. 10.

14 See, for example, *Partnership for Peace: Framework Document*,

http://www.mvp.hr/mvprh-www-eng/5-multilateral/pfp/pfp_framework.html.

15 'Interview: Jozo Rados, Minister of Defence of the Republic of Croatia', *Jane's Defence Weekly*, vol. 33, no. 16, 12 April 2000.

16 Kusovac, 'HDZ Tests Croat Coalition', p. 21.

17 'Croatian Government Sets Terms of Cooperation with the Hague', *RFE/RL Newsline*, 13 April 2000; 'Croatian Parliament Approves Hague Cooperation Statement', *ibid.*, 17 April 2000.

18 'Croatian President Fires Seven Generals', *ibid.*, 29 September 2000.

19 'Veterans End Protest in Croatia', *ibid.*, 28 March 2003.

20 Interviews, Ministry of Defence, Zagreb, July 2002.

21 'Croatian President Joins Bobetko Fray, Urges Cooperation with the Hague', *RFE/RL Newsline*, 26 September 2002; 'Croatian Conservatives Call for President's Impeachment', *ibid.*, 27 September 2002.

22 Interviews, Zagreb, July 2002.

23 Interviews, Zagreb, July 2002. These problems are compounded by the often tense relationship between the Ministry of Defence and the General Staff. Both organisations have departments whose work duplicates that of the other, yet officials observe that there is only limited contact between the two institutions and that the development of joint policy proposals almost never occurs. Interview with Dragan Lozancic, Ministry of Defence, Zagreb, 11 July 2002; interview with Brigadier Zvonimir Mahecic, Military

Cabinet of the Office of the President, Zagreb, 11 July 2002.

[24] Interview with Defence Minister Jozo Rados, Ministry of Defence, Zagreb, 10 July 2002. It is also important to observe that many of Rados's critics remain highly sceptical of these attempts to play down politicisation and patronage in the Ministry of Defence.

[25] Cottey et al. 'The Second Generation', pp. 35–36, 40.

[26] Alex J. Bellamy, 'A Revolution in Civil–Military Affairs: The Professionalisation of Croatia's Armed Forces', in Forster, Edmunds and Cottey (eds), *The Challenge of Military Reform in Postcommunist Europe: Building Professional Armed Forces*, pp. 176–77.

[27] Interview with officials in the Ministry of Defence, Zagreb, July 2002.

[28] Zunec, 'Democracy in the "Fog of War"', p. 227.

[29] Interview with General Pavao Miljavac, Parliamentary Committee for Internal Affairs and National Security, Zagreb, 9 July 2002.

[30] Interview with Miljavac.

[31] Interviews with parliamentarians and with officials in the Ministry of Defence, Zagreb, July 2002.

[32] Private communication, Zagreb, July 2002.

[33] Interview with Zunec. An exception to these trends include the introduction of a new course on Military Sociology and the Sociology of War at Zagreb University in 1995.

[34] Interview with Bozidar Javorovic, Director of the Centre for Defendological Research; Professor of Political Science, Zagreb University, Zagreb, 10 July 2002.

[35] Interview with Ozren Zunec, Professor of Sociology, Zagreb University, 9 July 2002.

[36] Interviews with Zunec, Mahecic and Vlatko Cvrtila, Professor of Political Science, Zagreb University, 11 July 2002.

[37] Interview with Cvrtila.

[38] Alex J. Bellamy, 'A Crisis of Legitimacy: Armed Forces and Society in Croatia', in Anthony Forster, Timothy Edmunds and Andrew Cottey (eds), *Soldiers and Societies in Postcommunist Europe: Legitimacy and Change* (Palgrave-Macmillan, forthcoming, 2003).

[39] Article 135, *Constitution of the Federal Republic of Yugoslavia*, 1992, http://www.vj.yu/english/en_odredbe.

[40] James Gow, 'The European Exception: Civil–Military Relations in the Federal Republic of Yugoslavia (Serbia and Montenegro)', in Cottey, Edmunds and Forster (eds), *Democratic Control of Armed Forces in Postcommunist Europe: Guarding the Guards*, p. 203.

[41] Robin Alison Remington, 'The Yugoslav Army: Trauma and Transition', in Danopoulos and Zirker (eds), *Civil–Military Relations in the Soviet and Yugoslav Successor States*, p. 167; Gow, 'The European Exception', pp. 201–20.

[42] Remington, 'The Yugoslav Army', p. 167; Gow, 'The European Exception', pp. 202–203.

[43] Gow, 'The European Exception', pp. 205–206.

[44] Milosevic cultivated a number of different special forces

groupings, which fell under different chains of command. Broadly, these comprised special police elements such as the JSO and the Special Force Police (PJP), and military special forces. The former were outside the VJ chain of command – normal or otherwise. The latter carried out much of their work with the military Counter-Intelligence Service (KOS), which in practice functioned as an autonomous military chain of command. The author is grateful to Witek Nowosielski for this point.

45 Gow, 'The European Exception', pp. 209–10; Budimir Babovic, 'Police as a Tool of Milosevic's Autocratic Rule', *In the Triangle of State Power: Army, Police, Paramilitary Units* (Belgrade: Helsinki Committee, 2001), pp. 24–31, http://www.helsinki.org.yu/doc/pubs/files/eng/HFiles9.zip.
46 James Gow and Ivan Zverzhanovski, 'Legitimacy and the Military Revisited: Civil–Military Relations and the Future of Yugoslavia', in Forster, Edmunds and Cottey (eds), *Soldiers and Societies in Postcommunist Europe: Legitimacy and Change.*
47 Under the new constitution, Serbia provides 95.5% of the defence budget, with the balance coming from Montenegro. Correspondence with Colonel Witek Nowosielski, UK Defence Attaché, Belgrade, 14 April 2003.
48 In Djukanovic's case, this was because he had no real stake in the VJ or its funding. For his part, Milutinovic was indicted by the ICTY in May 1999 and

has subsequently attempted to keep a low political profile.
49 Interviews at the Office of the President of the Federal Republic of Yugoslavia, Belgrade, June 2002.
50 Interview with Miroslav Filipovic, Member of the Foreign Policy Committee of the Federal Assembly of the FRY, 18 June 2002.
51 The Law came under particular criticism for subordinating KOS to the federal Ministry of Defence rather than the General Staff as is normal in most other countries. Interviews, Belgrade, June 2002.
52 See, for example, Philipp Fluri and Miroslav Hadzic, *Compendium of Yugoslav Laws on the Security Sector: Human Rights and Democratic Oversight Aspects* (Belgrade: Geneva Centre for the Democratic Control of Armed Forces and the Centre for Civil–Military Relations, 2002).
53 Article 56, *Constitution of the Republic of Serbia and Montenegro* (4 February 2003).
54 Miroslav Hadzic, 'New Constitutional Position of the Army', *CCMR Website*, http://www.ccmr-bg.org/analize/rec/word13.htm
55 *Arming Saddam: The Yugoslav Connection*, ICG Balkans Report No. 136, 3 December 2002, pp. 12–13.
56 'Washington Warns Belgrade over Arms Sales to Iraq'; 'As Yugoslav Government Meets in Emergency Session', *RFE/RL Newsline*, 23 October 2002.
57 'Supreme Defence Council Dismisses Army Intelligence Chief', *B92 News Archive*, 21 March 2003; 'Serbia and

Montenegro Sacks 16 Old Guard Officers', *RFE/RL Newsline*, 8 August 2003.

[58] The 2003 constitutional Charter stipulates that either constituent republic can call a referendum on complete independence after three years. Given that Montenegro retains a strong constituency in favour of independence, this remains a distinct possibility for 2006. Article 60, *The Constitutional Charter of the State Union of Serbia and Montenegro*, http://www.mfa.gov.yu/Facts/charter_e.html.

[59] For more on the DOS, see *Serbia's Transition: Reforms Under Siege*, ICG Balkans Report No. 117, 21 September 2001.

[60] Interview with James Lyon, Director, Serbia Project, International Crisis Group, 18 June 2002; *Belgrade's Lagging Reform: Cause for International Concern*, ICG Report No. 126, 7 March 2002, p. 14.

[61] *Human Rights in Transition: Serbia 2001*, Helsinki Committee for Human Rights in Serbia Annual Report 2001 (Belgrade: Helsinki Committee, 2002), http://www.helsinki.org.yu/report.php?lang=en.

[62] 'Yugoslav Defence Minister Quits', *RFE/RL Newsline*, 16 January 2002; 'Yugoslav Military Contradicts Foreign Minister', *ibid.*, 19 February 2002.

[63] *Serbia: Military Intervention Threatens Democratic Reform*, ICG Balkans Briefing, 28 March 2002, pp. 2–3. While Perisic has since been cleared on a legal technicality, many observers believe that the accusations against him were legitimate at the time and therefore justified

the actions of KOS. Moreover, there is also a body of opinion which believes that KOS was not acting on behalf of Pavkovic when it arrested Perisic. By March 2002, the relationship between Kostunica and Pavkovic had deteriorated; it was head of KOS and Kostunica ally General Aco Tomic who took the 'credit' for the arrest. Tomic is currently detained for questioning in connection with his contacts with organised crime. The author is grateful to Witek Nowosielski for this point.

[64] Interview with Colonel Nowosielski, UK Defence Attaché, Belgrade, 19 June 2002.

[65] 'Yugoslav Army Chief's Fate to be Determined', *RFE/RL Newsline*, 26 March 2002

[66] See *B92 News Archive*, 24, 25, 26 June 2002; 11, 12 July 2002, www.b92.net. Pavkovic has since been implicated in the assassination of Zoran Djindjic.

[67] Timothy Edmunds, 'A Turning Point in Yugoslavia's Civil–Military Relations?', *Journal of Defence Studies*, vol. 2, no. 2, Summer 2003.

[68] *Serbia: Military Intervention*, pp. 4–7.

[69] 'Allegations of Planned "Takeover" Gain Ground', *B92*, 27 June 2002. Kostunica denied these allegations and the affair blew over.

[70] 'Army Officers Abandon Sacked Leader', *ibid.*, 26 June 2002.

[71] Krga has not remained completely silent however. Indeed, in August 2003 as this paper was going to press he raised the possibility of a return of VSCG troops to Kosovo 'within the framework of UN

Security Council Resolution 1244 [on the situation relating to Kosovo]' in apparent contradiction of official government policy. His suggestion was later publicly downplayed by defence minister Tadic. 'Head of Serbia and Montenegro's Army Proposes Return of Armed Forces to Kosova', *RFE/RL Newsline*, 22 August 2003. 'Serbia and Montenegro's Defence Minister Doubts Return of Troops to Kosova', *ibid.*, 26 August 2003.

[72] Article 41, *Constitution of the Republic of Serbia and Montenegro*.

[73] Interview with Radovanovic.

[74] Interviews in Belgrade, November 2002.

[75] Interview with Momcilo Perisic, Chairman, Parliamentary Defence Committee of the Parliament of the Federal Republic of Yugoslavia, 18 June 2002.

[76] Interview with Filipovic.

[77] Interviews, Belgrade, June 2002.

[78] Boris Tadic, 'Reform of the Defense System of Serbia and Montenegro', *Statement by the Minister of Defence at the Assembly of Serbia and Montenegro*, Belgrade, 21 March 2003. In May 2003, the VSO confirmed that the General Staff would become a department of the Ministry of Defence. 'Civilian Control Over Serbia and Montenegro's Military Confirmed', *RFE/RL Newsline*, 7 May 2003.

[79] Tadic himself recognised this in his speech, providing a timeline for the implementation of the ten-point plan to 2010.

[80] Despite attempts to suppress it, civil society as a whole in Serbia remained dynamic and important throughout the Milosevic period, as evidenced by the proliferation of social movements and numerous occasions of civil disobedience. Nonetheless, the defence sector in FRY remained insular and largely closed to outside influences, though both CCMR and the G17 Institute were active in this area to a limited degree from 1997.

[81] Interviews, Belgrade, June and November 2002; www.ccmr-bg.org; www.helsinki.org.yu; www.g17plus.org.yu.

[82] Interview with Milorad Timotic, vice–president of CCMR, 17 November 2002; http://www.ccmr-bg.org/vesti/news.htm.

[83] Correspondence with Pavle Jankovic, Director, School of Security Sector Reform, G17 Institute, 7 February 2003.

Chapter 2

[1] Christopher Donnelly, 'Shaping Soldiers for the 21st Century', *NATO Review*, vol. 48, no. 2, Summer/Autumn 2000, pp. 28–31.

[2] *The Military Balance, 2002–03* (Oxford: Oxford University Press for the IISS, 2002), p. 69.

[3] Marinko Ogorec and Robert Baric, 'Republic of Croatia in Security Constellation of South Eastern Europe', unpublished paper, 2001; 'Defence Spending, Croatia', *Jane's Sentinel Security Assessment – the Balkans – p. 8*, 11 April 2001.

[4] Zoran Kusovac, 'Croatia To Reduce Forces By 40%', *Jane's Defence Weekly*, 6 February 2002.

5 Article 7, *Constitution of the Republic of Croatia.*

6 Interview with Zoran Milanovic, Ministry of Foreign Affairs, Zagreb, 9 July 2002; Interviews at the Ministry of Defence, Zagreb, July 2002.

7 Interview at the Ministry of Foreign Affairs, Zagreb, July 2002.

8 Timothy Edmunds, Anthony Forster and Andrew Cottey, 'Conclusions: Patterns and Trends in Military–Society Relations in Postcommunist Europe', in Forster, Edmunds and Cottey (eds), *Soldiers and Societies in Postcommunist Europe: Legitimacy and Change.*

9 See, for example, 'Fire Spreads on Croatian Island', *RFE/RL Newsline*, 13 August 2003.

10 Interviews at the Ministry of Defence, Zagreb, July 2002.

11 Interviews with Baric, Zunec and Lt.-Col. Richard Thornely, UK Defence Attaché, Zagreb, 8 July 2002.

12 Zvonimir Mahacic, 'Challenges of Reform and the Reduction of Croatia's Armed Forces: Politics of Personnel Management as a Consequence of War Events and the Establishment of Croatia's Armed Forces', paper presented at the conference 'Wars of Former Yugoslavia: The Sociology of Armed Conflict at the Turn of the Millennium', 6-8 December, Zagreb 2002.

13 For example, one analyst confided in 2002 that 'on a good day' only four of the HRZ's 28 MiG–21bis fighter aircraft were serviceable. Private communication, Zagreb, July 2002.

14 Interviews, Zagreb, July 2002.

15 Bellamy, 'A Revolution in Civil–Military Affairs', p. 175; correspondence with Zunec.

16 *CIA World Fact Book: Croatia,* http://www.cia.gov/cia/publications/factbook/geos/hr.html#Econ.

17 Interviews at the Ministry of Defence, Zagreb, July 2002.

18 Kusovac, 'HDZ Tests Croat Coalition', p. 20.

19 Interview with Zunec.

20 Private communication, London, 24 October 2002.

21 Interview with Brigadier Zvonimir Mahecic, Military Cabinet of the Office of the President of Croatia, London, 28 October 2002.

22 Adam Roberts, *Nations in Arms: The Theory and Practice of Territorial Defence* (London: Chatto and Windus, 1977) pp. 124–217; Gow, *Legitimacy and the Military*, pp. 45–50.

23 Bellamy, 'A Revolution in Civil–Military Affairs', pp. 172–173.

24 Interviews with Zunec and Milanovic.

25 Kristan J. Wheaton, 'Cultivating Croatia's Military', *NATO Review*, Summer/Autumn 2000, pp. 11–12.

26 *Ibid.*, pp. 11–12.

27 Interview with Kozlica.

28 Interviews with Cvrtila and Javorovic.

29 Private communications, Zagreb, July 2002.

30 *Politika*, 5 January 2003, in 'Krga Has Been Appointed Chief of AY General Staff', *CCMR Press Review*, www.ccmr-bg.org/vesti/frommedia/media0027print.htm; Tadic, 'Reform of the Defense System'.

31 Article 133, *Constitution of the Federal Republic of Yugoslavia*, 27 April 1992.

[32] Gow, 'Professionalisation and the Yugoslav Army', pp. 189–90.

[33] Article 53, *Constitution of the Republic of Serbia and Montenegro*.

[34] *Politika*, 5 January 2003.

[35] *Ibid.*, 29 December 2002, in 'Krga Has Been Appointed'; correspondence with Nowosielski.

[36] 'A Peacekeeping Mission for Serbia and Montenegro?', *RFE/RL Newsline*, 6 August 2003.

[37] The VJ was widely perceived to have performed well in this operation and won praise from both NATO and the OSCE. Gow, 'Professionalisation', pp. 190–92; *Peace in Preševo: Quick Fix or Long Term Solution*, ICG Report No. 116, 10 August 2001, p. 17

[38] Interviews, Belgrade, June and November 2002.

[39] As illustrated by the decision to transfer the task of border protection from the army to the republican interior ministries.

[40] Radic, 'Modernisation of the Yugoslav Army'.

[41] 'Army – Yugoslavia', *Jane's Sentinel Security Assessment – The Balkans* (11 February 2003); Correspondance with Nowosielski.

[42] Interview with Vladan Zivulovic, President, Atlantic Council of Yugoslavia, 26 June 2002.

[43] It is significant that General Krga himself has called these changes 'restructuring and not reform'. He has stressed that for real reform to take place, the army must wait for the approval of a National Security Strategy that in turn would lead to a coherent Defence Doctrine and Reform Plan. Branko Krga, *Statement to the International Seminar 'Armed Forces Reform: Experiences and Challenges'*, Belgrade, 18 November 2002; Interviews, Belgrade, June 2002.

[44] Estimated figures. *The Military Balance 1997–98 to 2001–02* (London: International Institute for Strategic Studies, 1997–2001).

[45] 'Yugoslav Army to Send Troops Home to Save Food Rations', *RFE/RL Newsline*, September 2002.

[46] Radic, 'Modernisation of the Yugoslav Army'.

[47] Interviews, Belgrade, November 2002.

[48] *Danas*, 27 November 2002, in 'Still Facing Serious Reforms in the Army of Yugoslavia' *CCMR Press Review*, www.ccmr-org.bg/vesti/frommedia.media0027print.htm; *Politika*, 5 January 2003; interviews, Belgrade, December 2002.

[49] Radic, 'Modernisation of the Yugoslav Army'.

[50] Interview with Miroslav Hadzic, quoted in Zoran Kusovac, 'Belgrade's Battle for Change', *Jane's Defence Weekly*, 16 January 2002, p. 23.

[51] Tadic, 'Reform of the Defense System'. See also 'Interview with Boris Tadic', *Jane's Defence Weekly*, 16 July 2003, p. 32.

[52] Interview with Nowosielski; Gow, 'Professionalisation', p. 186.

[53] 'Military Schools', *Website of the Yugoslav Army*, www.vj.yu/english/en_obrazovanje/index.htm.

[54] Gow, 'Professionalisation', pp. 187–88.

[55] Tadic, 'Reform of the Defense System'.

Chapter Three

[1] 'Purposes and Principles of Enlargement', *Study on NATO Enlargement*, September 1995, http://www.nato.int/docu/basictxt/enl-9502.htm.

[2] *Partnership for Peace: Framework Document*, 10 January 1994, http://www.nato.int/pfp/pfp.htm.

[3] 'The Partnership for Peace Planning and Review Process', *NATO Handbook 2001*, http://www.nato.int/docu/handbook/2001/hb030208.htm; Frank Boland, 'Mapping the Future', *NATO Review*, vol. 50, no. 1, Spring 2002.

[4] MPRI Website, European activities section, http://www.mpri.com/subchannels/int_europe.html.

[5] Another interpretation of the US/MPRI/Croatia relationship is that it was part of a deal between Tudjman and the US government over Croatian activities in Bosnia. According to this argument, Croatia was offered concrete (though indirect) military assistance though MPRI in return for abandoning its support for the Croatian Herzeg–Bosna and accepting the Croat–Muslim federation instead. Biljana Vankovska, 'Privatisation of Security and Security Sector Reform in Croatia', in Damian Lilly and Michael von Tangen Page (eds), *Security Sector Reform: The Challenges and Opportunities of the Privatisation of Security* (London: International Alert, September 2002), p. 70.

[6] Stuart McGhie, 'Private Military Companies: Soldiers, Inc.', *Jane's Defence Weekly*, 22 May 2002.

[7] Vankovska, 'Privatisation of Security'.

[8] Wheaton, 'Cultivating Croatia's Military'. The United States held a four-day joint military exercise with the Croatian Air Force in Croatia on 13–16 May 2002.

[9] Interview with Lozancic.

[10] Interviews, Zagreb, July 2002.

[11] Interviews at the Ministry of Defence, Zagreb, July 2002.

[12] Interview with Thornely.

[13] Interviews, Zagreb, July 2002. See also Foreign Minister Tonino Picula in his speech to NATO foreign ministers on Croatia's accession to PFP in May 2000, where he couched the importance of the moment in terms of civilisational values. See *Opening Statement*, NATO Foreign Minister's Meeting, Florence, Italy, 24–25 May 2000, http://www.nato.int/docu/speech/2000/s000525f.htm.

[14] Wheaton, 'Cultivating Croatia's Military'.

[15] Interview with Zoran Milanovic, Ministry of Foreign Affairs, Zagreb, 9 July 2002; interview with Petar Mihatov, Ministry of Foreign Affairs, Zagreb, 11 July 2002.

[16] Interviews, Zagreb, July 2002.

[17] Interview with Lozancic.

[18] Interview with Bozidar Javorovic, Professor of Political Science, University of Zagreb, 10 July 2002.

[19] Interview with Milanovic. Levels of popular support for NATO declined significantly in the wake of the US-led war with Iraq in 2003. Correspondence with Zunec.

[20] Bellamy, '"Like Drunken Geese in the Fog"', p. 189.

21 'Croatian Government Refuses To Hand Over War Crimes Suspect'; 'As Prime Minister Equates Aging General's Actions with "Struggle for Independence"', *RFE/RL Newsline*, 24 September 2002; 'Croatia Seeks to Challenge the Indictment of General Bobetko', *ibid.*, 30 September 2002.

22 'EU Calls on Croatia to Cooperate with the Hague', *ibid.*, 1 October 2002; 'NATO Calls on Croatia To Extradite General Bobetko', *ibid.*, 3 October 2002; 'Croatian President Says General Bobetko Should Go To the Hague; *ibid.*, 16 October 2002; 'EU Gives Croatia the Brush-Off', *ibid.*, 6 November 2002.

23 'Controversial Croatian General Hospitalized', *ibid.*, 14 November 2002; 'Croatian Prime Minister Defends His "Humanitarian Gesture"', *ibid.*, 15 November 2002

24 'Hague Doctors Rule Croatian General Unfit for Trial', *ibid.*, 3 February 2003.

25 Interviews with Zvonimir Mahcic, Veselko Grubisic, Croatian Delegation to NATO; Mario Horvatic, Croatian Delegation to NATO, London, 28 October 2002.

26 'Hague Tribunal Wants To Interview Three More Croats', *RFE/RL Newsline*, 6 November 2002; 'Croatian Government Passes Along Request By War Crimes Tribunal', *ibid.*, 19 November 2002.

27 'Controversial Croatian Judge Frees Eight After War Crimes Acquittal', *ibid.*, 25 November 2002.

28 'Veterans End Protest in Croatia'.

29 Interview with Zivulovic; 'Yugoslav and NATO Officials Meet in Secret', *RFE/RL Newsline*, 14 May 2002.

30 Correspondence with Nowosielski, 10 March 2003.

31 Interview with Grp. Capt. (rtd.) Angus Morris, Defence Advisory Team, UK Ministry of Defence, 22 August 2003. While details have yet to be confirmed, at the time of writing the advisor appears set to take up his position in late 2003.

32 Interview with Morris, 11 March 2003. The US authorised military assistance to Serbia-Montenegro in May 2003. 'US President Approves Military Aid to Serbia and Montenegro', *RFE/RL Newsline*, 7 May 2003.

33 'Yugoslavia: Report on Security Sector Reform', *DCAF Press Release*, 14 December 2001, http://www.dcaf.ch/news/press_releases/Belgrade/FRY.PressRelease-E.pdf.

34 The DCAF/EWI report was not circulated widely and very few of its recommendations were acted on. The report itself was criticised by some in Belgrade, who suggested that it was an inappropriate use of scarce resources and that a better job could have been done by local experts. Miroslav Lazanski, quoted in *Human Rights in Transition: Serbia 2001*.

35 Interview with Morris.

36 Interviews, Belgrade, November 2002.

37 Krga, *Statement to the International Seminar*; Tadic, 'Reform of the Defense System'; 'Defense Minister Calls for Integration of Serbia and Montenegro in NATO', *RFE/RL*

Newsline, 22 April 2003; 'General Says Serbia and Montenegro Ready for Partnership for Peace', *ibid.*, 24 April 2003; 'Interview with Boris Tadic'.

[38] 'Yugoslavia Seeks Membership of Partnership for Peace', *ibid.*, 26 April 2002 .

[39] Serbia and Montenegro was finally admitted to the CoE on 3 April 2003; 'Council of Europe To Admit Serbia and Montenegro', *ibid.*, 27 March 2003.

[40] Interview with Nowosielski.

[41] 'Yugoslav Army To Cut Off Military Aide to Bosnian Serb Army', *RFE/RL Newsline*, 8 February 2002; Yugoslavia Approves the Dayton Agreement', *ibid.*, 18 December 2002. See also, 'Belgrade Ends Military Links to Banja Luka', *ibid.*, 9 April 2003.

[42] 'Yugoslav Army Chief's Fate To Be Determined'; 'And Yugoslav Leaders Suggest Joining NATO's Partnership for Peace', *ibid.*, 26 March 2002.

[43] Interviews, Belgrade, November 2002.

[44] See, for example, 'Yugoslav Army Must Be Reformed for Closer NATO Ties', *RFE/RL Newsline* 23 May 2002; and 'Room for Yugoslavia in NATO Says Robertson', *B92*, 31 January 2003.

[45] Predrag Simic, 'Security Sector Reform in Yugoslavia', in Timothy Edmunds (ed.), *Security Sector Reform in Croatia and Yugoslavia* (London: IISS, 2003).

[46] Interviews with Radovanovic and Mijalkovski; interviews, Belgrade, November 2002.

[47] See, for example, 'US Group Says Only One Man Stands Between Serbia and NATO',

RFE/RL Newsline, 15 July 2003.

[48] Gow, *The Serbian Project*, pp. 75–79.

[49] The decision to extradite Milosevic to The Hague on 28 June 2001 occurred in the context of an aid donor's conference for FRY on 29 June 2001. Both the US and EU had made it plain to the Yugoslav authorities that a substantial aid package amounting to $1.28 billion in grants and loans would be at risk if the extradition did not take place.

[50] 'Yugoslav Parliament Passes Controversial Hague Cooperation Law', *RFE/RL Newsline*, 12 April 2002; 'Belgrade Gives War Criminals Deadline', *ibid.*, 18 April 2002.

[51] 'Yugoslav Court Issues Arrest Warrants for War Criminals', *ibid.*, 9 May 2002; 'Milosevic's Top General Joins Him in the Hague', *ibid.*, 25 April 2002.

[52] 'US Lifts Freeze on Aid to Yugoslavia', *ibid.*, 22 May 2002.

[53] 'US Calls for Strict Cooperation with the War Crimes Tribunal', *ibid.*, 3 January 2003.

[54] Correspondence with Nowosielski; 'US Calls on Serbia To Arrest Indicted War Criminals'; 'After Serbian Leaders Visit the Hague', *ibid.*, 3 April 2003; 'Chief War Crimes Prosecutor Hails New Era of Cooperation with Serbia and Montenegro', *ibid.*, 20 May 2003; 'Serbian Police Arrest War Crimes Suspect Amid Violent Clashes', *ibid.*, 13 June 2003.

[55] Biljana Vankovska, 'The Military–Society Relationship in a Conflict Milieu: Practice Re-examined and Theory Revised', in Marie Vlachova and Marina Caparini (eds), *Military Society Relations in Countries of*

Transition (Belgrade: DCAF and CCMR, forthcoming, 2003).

[56] See, for example, *Serbia: Military Intervention*, pp. 4–6.

[57] 'Mladic without Yugoslav Army Security', *B92*, 26 March 2002.

[58] Interviews, Belgrade, June 2002.

[59] In the second round of the Serbian presidential elections in December 2002, the extreme nationalist Vojislav Sesel, who was subsequently indicted by The Hague, achieved a substantial 36.3% of the vote.

[60] Interviews, Belgrade, November 2002.

Conclusion

[1] The unit directly involved in the assassination – the JSO – has been disbanded and several of its members placed in police custody on charges connected both to the assassination of Djindjic and the 2000 murder of former Serbian President Ivan Stambolic. 'Serbian Police Arrest Alleged Assassin', *RFE/RL Newsline*, 26 March 2003.

[2] Tadic, 'Reform of the Defense System'.

For Product Safety Concerns and Information please contact our
EU representative GPSR@taylorandfrancis.com Taylor & Francis
Verlag GmbH, Kaufingerstraße 24, 80331 München, Germany